Off the Hozzle

53rd State Press

Chicago, Illinois

53SP 08
October, 2011

ISBN 978-0-9817533-7-9
Library of Congress Control Number: 2011937935

53rd State Press
Chicago, Illinois
www.53rdstatepress.org

Rob Erickson

Off the Hozzle

illustrated by Bob Erickson

53rd State Press

Chicago, Illinois

"Lumberob is a terrible witch doctor. You've seen the forest in which he works his dark sono-linguistic magic, but only from the outside. Enter its interior, and you will be ecstatically sorry." – *Sibyl Kempson, playwright*

"Behind the manic repetitions and surrealist hijinks lies an earnest exploration of one of the most powerful monomanias known to man: golf addiction. Erickson understands the heart and mind of the golfer, knows the history of the game and its players, and has more than a passing acquaintance with golf's mind-blowing catalogue of instructional doctrine. If this won't cure your slice, nothing will. Actually... nothing will." – *Tom Dunne, golf writer*

"One feels as if one is learning to understand language anew, as if one is just discovering that sounds and movements are distinct, that they can come apart and be rejoined in different patterns. It feels as if one is not remembering so much as lost in a noodling corridor of the brain in which the memories are stored. What is amazing is, of course, that this is just a play about golf." – *Matthew Noah Smith, Assistant Professor of Philosophy, Yale University*

"A manic pinball game of scattergun language, non-sequitur narrative, and spring-loaded physicality."– *Rob Marcato, Artistic Line Producer at Signature Theater*

"Watching Rob perform *Off the Hozzle* for the first time reminded us of many of our best experiences in seeing our friend Richard Lewis. The narrative slides into the surreal and we are taken into an alternative universe of frenetic, exciting hilarity." – *Jon and Lou Dembrow, connoisseurs at large, Soho Rep Board Chair and filmmaker, respectively*

"Artists of the world, listen to this: you have nothing to lose but your equilibrium. Throughout his music there is a lyric impulse, a rising of the heart, a moral passion that represents the spirit of the millennium at its best. At the same time, Lumberob's music is exceedingly rigorous; he has the optimism of his generation without its willed naiveté." – *Anne Gridley, actor and totally hot babe (her words)*

"Rob has created a character so original it transcends classification." – *J. C. Chandor, filmmaker*

"He's a major talent." – *Jad Fair, musician and paper-cutter*

"Erickson's *Hozzle* shanks itself and us. The miss is mythic, and Eldrick no doubt swears at Erickson in his dreams for the hozzle's curse. *Off the Hozzle*'s drift is like that of history: One damn thing after another. I have no idea what a hozzle is, and don't think anyone does. Do you? I doubt it. Erickson's drift, however, is one of the most exciting around. One damn thing after another, and strangely we are not left behind. This work is worth every penny. Even Eldrick Woods wd say so."– *Mac Wellman, playwright and dark lord*

"Lumberob's music is the most intoxicating and addictive drug available." – *Pavol Liska, director and choreographer, Nature Theater of Oklahoma*

"Lumberob's performances turn ordinary men into giants. I never leave without feeling that I have survived a gentle emergency. All students of astronomy are made stronger; all customers become people."– *Amber Reed & Justin Jamail, ex-patriot poets and advocates*

"Rob has a ferocity that is captivating, intense, dizzy. We cannot stop looking at him, and then the unique rhythms get all flustery, stuck inside us and lock. He demands engagement. We can't help it." – *Dana Edell, PhD, theater director, designer, producer, and postdoctoral badass.*

"There's LUMBEROB – he's the best band around. He's like Aphex Twin meets Bobby McFerrin. He's like a one man party in your mouth. In the mouth of your ear."–*Vernon Chatman & John Lee, writers*

"Try and imagine your mouth was your hand, and you could do card tricks with it. Or try and imagine your mouth was your feets and it knew how to time step. Lumberob will flat out rearrange your DNA."– *Jeffrey M. Jones, playwright and gentleman provocateur*

"This piece obliterates language and leaves behind something glowing, amazing and altogether better than that which it has so lovingly destroyed. I was truly unprepared for how profoundly transformatively a dadaesque monologue about a golf swing would affectivate my neuro-psychological processes. When you see something this utterly original, the cynic in you wonders, 'Why is literally every single other person in the world so damn boring?' but then your super positive inner self emerges triumphant, asks the negative you to dance, and hefts all your fractured selves onto the astral plane, where spinning and flipping like crazed acrobats they bask in the glorious suspended moment of true inspiration and beauty that is *Off the Hozzle*. Probably one of the better golf plays you will encounter this year. Rob Erickson will do it to you in your mindhole."– *Brian Perkins, children's entertainer and daytime Emmy nominee*

"Lumberob taught me everything I know about measuring greens, intersecting vectors, inclination, slice, sweet spots and, I think, hypnotization? What was I saying? – *Jeff Penn, lawyer and father*

"He speaks words that flow or spurt out of him in an order that I don't think even he is prepared for and images emerge and combine with more images and a story forms and he takes us forward and sideways and underways until we reach the end and that first breath you take in will only make you want to scream for more. Then if you're lucky, he will inexplicably throw himself against the wall and start in again until what he is doing is fully realized, like an arch? Like a circle? I don't know like what and that's just it, it's like nothing you will ever know and at the same time it is absolutely right and brings you pure joy in all of his sincerity and weirdness. Lumberob behaves badly." – *Scott Adkins, writer and slumlord*

"This show made me happier than is allowed by most people." – *Cara Marcous, writer/producer*

Off the Hozzle was originally produced, performed, and written as part of a residency at Dixon Place in New York City in May and June of 2008.

Written, directed, and designed by Rob Erickson
Performed by lumberob
Produced by Leslie Strongwater
Lit by Liz Jenetopulous
Assisted by Alexandra Ruhland-Syquia

Off the Hozzle was also performed live on WFMU's Acousmatic Theater Hour with Jason G and Karinne in January of 2009.

((archived at http://wfmu.org/playlists/shows/30131))

Table of Contents

INTRODUCTION

by Leslie Strongwater

Disclosure: The play that you have in your hands is a mad pinging fury and it needs some room. You will need to let it unravel slowly as it gathers steam. Mesmerized, you will follow it for a time, and it will lose you in a puff of smoke. I promise, if you listen, it will find you, find you in your mind.

I was given the chance to see this play take shape at Dixon Place, the laboratory theater, where Rob developed, dissected and re-sculpted his script in residency on the Bowery from May to June of 2008. Ellie Covan's living room, as Dixon Place was known, had seen the likes of over 20 years of hybridized performance art, and specialized in providing a safe haven for the avant-garde. Technically, it was a simple show: one mic, one blackout, some golf theory, and seven levels of tension. Are we going to get hit? Is it going to get loud? Did I really pay $12 for this?

Rob was nothing if not disciplined, hurtling ideas off the old coffered ceiling until he was literally breathless, transforming the intimate space until it felt both vast and secure. His 1½ year-old daughter, muse-like, played with old theater junk in the corner, couch cushions and clip-lamps; her developing language and behavior served to expand Rob's already electric palette. Stop. Start. We weren't dealing with a set of randomized words; this was full-blown fixation. Infectious repetition. Flow. Impossibly, as if under duress, Rob squeezed more words into words. He was a speedball, adhering and reacting fast to the ricochets of his own structure. Had I been able to, I would have turned the second extension of his show into an on-going engagement.

Off the Hozzle marked the only use of deer netting in the theater and one of the first plays I watched where I thought perhaps I had been slipped something, something good. His ear then, as now, is finely tuned for eccentric, unsettling aural patterns, sly rhythms, encapsulated best by Jacques Lecoq's concept of 'complicité,' closely related to a sense of dark play or collusive spirit. *Off the Hozzle* is as it sounds. Like you are losing your mind.

There are certain lines from plays that make their way unbeknownst into their hosts' subconscious...lines that trickle in and out during (in)opportune moments. Many will come and go unnoticed, unaware of their naissance and unafraid of eventual obsolescence.

You will come to know this play and feel its hold, unlike anything you've ever eaten or slept with. It will stick you (like a pig) and squeeze you (like a ripe Florida grapefruit). Give in and don't bother asking why.

Just figure out when you can go again, man.

PREFACE

by Rob Erickson

Let's say it is early on a Saturday morning in 1983, maybe 1984. My father is conducting a golf clinic for twenty or thirty fancy snowbirds. I am eight maybe nine years old. I linger nearby on the driving range, listening, giggling as my dad flails about wildly. He is most likely showing how to not swing the club. I have my own bucket of balls, and I patiently hit practice shots, perhaps working on working the ball a certain way. I understand how to practice, understand how to be productive, how to make progress. I am waiting for my cue. There it is.

Let's say my dad calls me over and introduces me to the group. They greet me rather warmly: "How adorable!" or "Gracious, I bet he can really hit it!" Well, I hit a few shots, mostly to gain their trust – probably nice high easy-going nine irons.

Let's say I do have a beautiful golf swing. Next, my dad starts the lesson and rolls out some of the basic fundamentals of the golf swing. I follow along closely,slowly demonstrating proper positions. I serve as model, as visual aid. It is golden! They go goo-goo for me.

Let's say I learned to walk with a golf club in my hand.

Let's say this is a refined transcription of a text deformed in the air.

Let's say I like to stand up like a stand-up, but I am no stand-up.

Let's say I hold a microphone, and I plug it into some pedals, three pedals: an Akai Headrush, a Z.Vex Fuzz Factory, and a plain ol' brown BOSS Octave.

Let's say I'd love you to seek out my sound: vimeo/lumberob or lumberob/audio.

Let's say I play a show which I call lumberob. Maybe it's a character. Maybe it's an act.

Let's say it's a vocal show. Lumberob is a vocal show, a basic form of lo-fi phrase looping.

Let's say I play urgently overflowing glottal warbling, gagging, barking, toasting illegible.

Let's say I was a carpenter previous to my career as a middle school teacher.

Let's say I used to drive a big ass Suburban truck, so when we needed wood, at the job site, the refrain from the supervisor was often "Lumber, Rob!" and I would go.

Let's say you'll find six or seven of these (((sound: …))) in the text. What are you to do? Let's say when you happen upon these (((sound: …))) interruptions, you must stomp and clap and toss the book against a wall, or toss it into a twirling ceiling fan, yup! That's what you do.

or, Let's say you should imagine (((sound: …))) as a sound doubling tripling lurching unruly.

Let's say I write in the air, listening hearing thinking… shanking digressive.

Let's say Pete Mankins told me the original owl and the rooster tale. I mangled it.

Let's say this text is heavily influenced by the teachings of Bob Erickson, PGA professional.

Let's say this text is heavily illustrated by the pen and ink of Bob Erickson, my dad.

Let's say I am familiar with the late Homer Kelley's *The Golfing Machine*, nutty and rich.

Let's say together, "it's just a game."

Let's say this play here should be read aloud.

Let's say the pirate jokes must be read with a salty lilt.

Let's say I need to thank Leslie and Karinne and the SHM, and my mom.

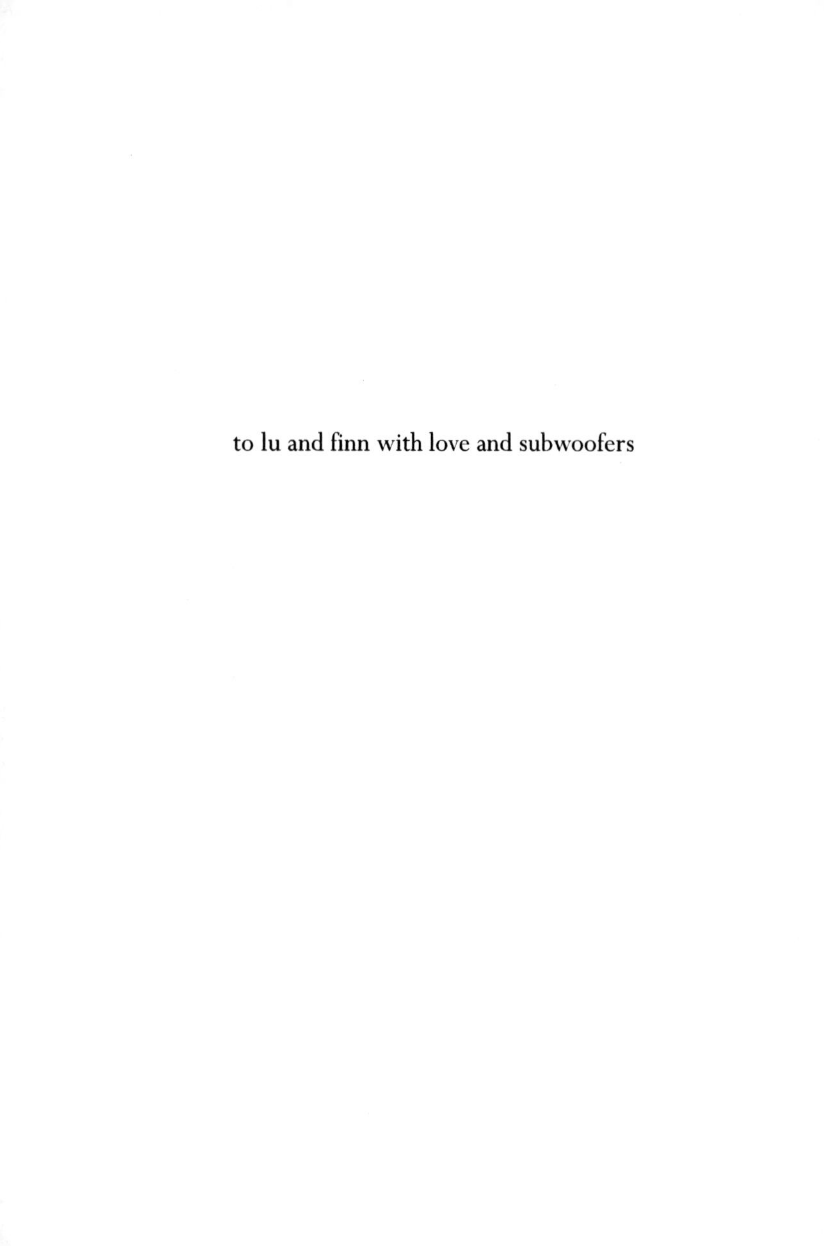

to lu and finn with love and subwoofers

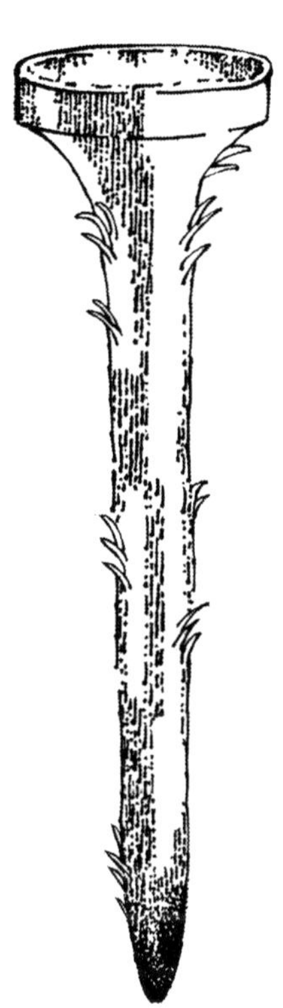

Oh girl! there, there is a point when you fix on something. Medium Cadet. there's there's a point when you fix on something like right, like right here.

pony says nneee. puppy says rruff. kitty says miaow.

I am I am certain of the ball. looks looks looks like this. it surprises you, yes. it surprises you. it makes, it's more than a more than a myth. there it is. it's more than a miss. there it is.

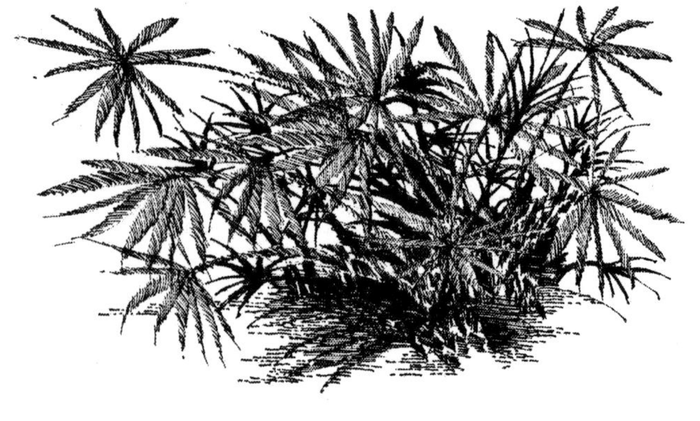

1.

Shanking itself. shanking itself is when, is when the ball hits off the hosel and it's it's more than a miss. it could go as many as ninety degrees off target, the target being the target you chose. you chose a target, you choose a target, and then well shanking itself is when it's a shot, it's a shot, it's a shot that's off like this and you and you chose it, you choose the target and the results the results are like this, like this, see?

and but understand they choose you, they choose you. perhaps you, perhaps you have been you have perhaps been benefit fitting or gaining, there's a gaining a gaining of confidence, a coupling of intention when you are chosen. questions begin to arise you know: are you, as a player, are you tired? are you tired of people suggesting that you're sandbagging when, or are you tired of people suggesting that you're a sandbagger when when when you know you really know you do indeed suck that bad?

after I was chosen, questions began to fly, like these questions began to fly and and real questions like these really got me going, got me going, got me got me on my long haul got me on my long haul my long haul.

in one day, in one day I played a full four, in one day, in one sun cycle, I played a full four rounds walking. that's seventy-two that's four that's four rounds of eighteen holes, eighteen times four, I played seventy-two holes walking so so when I was crossing from my seventh nine to my eighth side of nine, so my seventh, I am on the ninth hole finishing that nine which was my seventh nine moving across from nine to ten, moving across in front of the halfway house to the tenth hole which would be the start of my eighth nine, crossing from my seventh nine to my eighth nine, my eighth side of nine, so that would be my sixty-third hole, finishing finishing my seventh nine moving to my eighth nine which would be my sixty-third hole, seven times nine is, moving to my sixty-fourth hole crossing,

I now you yes you, I have to cross from nine to ten walking you have to cross in front of the halfway house, half of the way, I was walking from my sixty-third to my sixty-fourth hole in front of the halfway house you know from that last hole to the next hole. I didn't have time to stop at the halfway house. I'd actually spent, you know, I'd used up all my change earlier in the day. I walked up to the tenth tee and teed teed the ball up, teed the ball up and chose I chose the driver. I remember I remember looking back, looking back toward the halfway house.

for me it starts with a bell, it starts always starts started with a bell. even the first time it started it started with a bell. this is when I first met them yes this is first when. I was worn down. I was worn down that day crossing from my seventh from the ninth hole to my eighth to the tenth tee crossing in front of the halfway house.

(((sound: footsteps and tongueclicks go fft fft tck tck)))

for me it starts with a bell for me, tends to start, it did start as I was crossing in front of the halfway house, I heard a bell, I heard a bell coming coming perhaps from behind the halfway house at first, perhaps coming up from behind the halfway house but then realizing, I realized that this bell is a ringing bell is a bell ringing, realized it's ringing as if from everywhere all at once this bell this bell all at once this bell bell

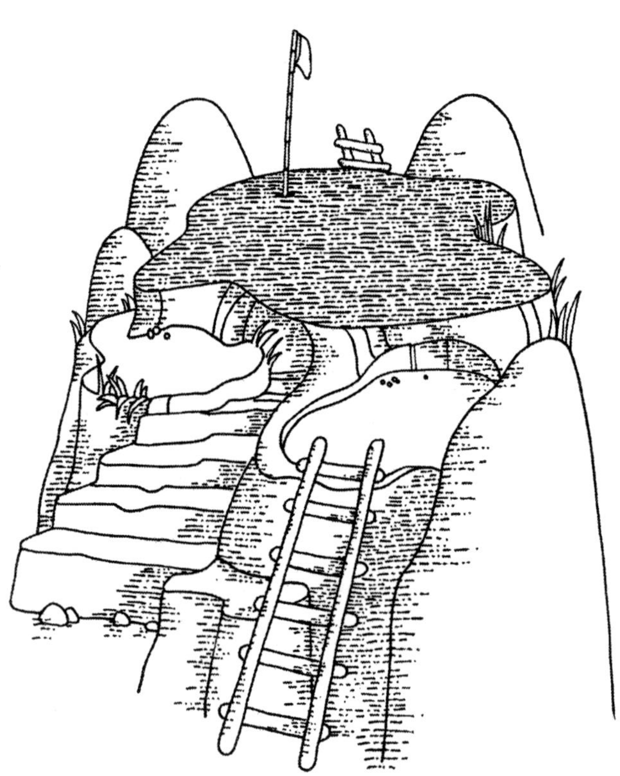

it started with, starts with this bell like this, it looks, it sounds, it rings ding dong, no there's more, it rings ding ding ding ding dong dong dong dong dong, no no not like that, like bonk donka donk donk bonk donka donk donk, no no not like that, more like a dinner bell like dikka dikka dikka dikka dikka dikka dikka or like this dinga dinga dinga dinga dinga dinga dinga dinga. oh yes, bells ding, don't they? ringing bells ding don't they ding? dingadingadinga dingadinga ding ding, no no, not like that, this was slower like gadingka dingk dingk gadinkga ding ding, yes kind of way.

call it MeetingTime. like this, like this what's happening now. this this connection, this sounding out sounds like sounds like this computer age this age now I always wondered about that bell, a mechanical bell leaves much to consider. there is always much to consider. this bell is well rounded, and his writing became sound, a belling like this, like this is what's happening now. this connection, this sounding out sounds like sounds like a worry, I would say it was a thinking sound.

we're talking say now thinking about acceleration. can you really punch harder? or can you only punch faster? an address position if not an entire address routine from start to finish in the beginning, yes? angular forces, aiming point, aiming points. there's always arcs and angles and an aiming point. there's an arc of attack. there's associated planes, maybe the floor or the door. there's a floor and there's a door.

there's an axe handle rope handle or an axe or a rope handle depending really depending if you are chopping or dragging something. I chop and I drag and I handle it. there's a certain tilt to it, an axis tilt. there's backspin sort of like throwing a frisbee on the zont zont. hori-zontal, no it is more like throwing a frisbee on the vert on the vert vert. vertical. there it is. it is substantial backspin sort like throwing it into forward reverse now.

there's balance. there's an idea of perfect balance, true balance, as if as if we're not always internally moving, as if balance is true stasis, a static, a stillness, as if we're not always moving, already over tipping. there's a check rein action. you know you have a leash you have a dog you have a check rein action. you've a leash you've a dog, you have check rein action, you might check rein check rein, you might have check rein action. there's club head lag, club head throwaway, there's release aways. there's efficient use, a multiplier, or there's a coefficient of restitution much like splashing water.

there's concentration, there's a certain concentration. there's an endless belt effect, there's the moving always endless concentration, the moving of a belt on a track, there's the endless belt, and an effect, the effect of the belt, there's the ratta-tat-tat-atat-tat at a shooting range like ducks going round the belt like an endless belt effect, the moving always, the shot shoots rat-tat-tat, the shots shoot ratta-tat-tat.

there's club head lag, club head throwaway. there's flat vertical wrist, there's vertical flat left wrist. yes there's flying wedges yes flying wedges much like multiple sails on a sailboat, gyroscopic action. there's a hinge. there's hinge action. there's hitting. there's swinging. the difference between the difference between between the difference between hitting and swinging, yes you and you might have a sling you know, you might hunt with a sling you might, you might, at home you might hunt with a sling you might, you might have a catapult? you might have a catapult at home? the difference between a sling and a catapult is tension, the tense presence in the pausing, the string, the stringing, the release, or the cutting will pop, it pops, a tense string pops. snaps.

there's ten pins. I love a game of ten pins! there's bowling. I love a game of ten pins, but where's the impact? ultimately, there's impact. well, there's impact in the game, the ball hits the pins, but is the impact the moment of the ball hitting the pins or is the impact, as it relates to your body, your hands, your fingers, is the impact the moment of you actually actually releasing, actually releasing the ball? there's release, there's thinking, there's thinking about what relates to your body, your body, your impact. there's billiards there is. there's billiards there's, I have some beanbags. I have a beanbag.

there's a dart on a dartboard. there's inclined planes. there's a pitched roof. there's laws, there's laws, we're talking thinking about levers, there's lever assemblies. there's a nutcracker. you might have a nutcracker at home. you have walking, you have running, you know you do. you pivot, you have a pivot center. there's a pivot center, there's tetherball round the pole. I like a game of tetherball. I enjoy, I enjoy very much a game of tetherball. you

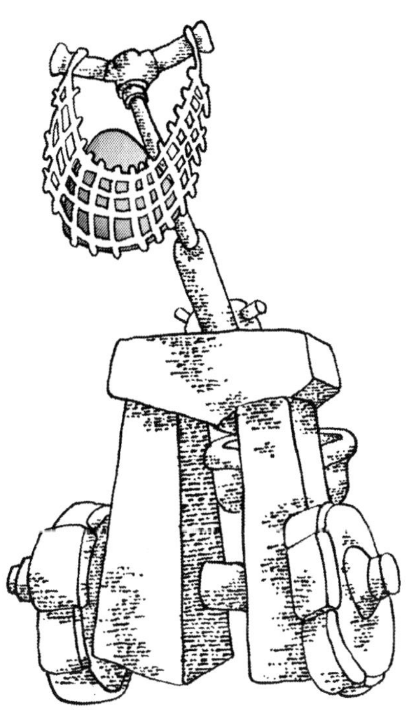

have, you have tetherball. there are very interesting lines in tetherball. there's kinetic, there's potential energy. there are lines. there's power accumulation. there's resultant force. there's power accumulation resultant forces much like you skip skipping, like skip skip, like skip skip skipping a rock skip skip skipping a rock across water. there's rhythm, there's a rhythm.

there's takeaway. there's throwaway, but first there's takeaway. there's right forearm drawing a line. there's right forearm drawing a line toward your stationary head, there's a stationary head much like a spinning skater has a head, oh I just love a game of rolling the hoop! you roll a hoop? I like rolling a hoop. there's a stationary head during a game of roll the hoop when you're steering, you need to be steering a rolling hoop, so you need a stationary head like a spinning skater has a stationary head when running clearly when you're steering a game of rolling the hoop clearly you're running, so there's running and walking, but a spinning skater is not running but spinning stationary. there's concentration. there's a stroke pattern. there's concentration, a distilling thought, still I'm thinking, always moving, thinking about concentration.

there are ingredients. we all have them, ingredients. there's a sweet spot. there's plumb-bob, there's plum-bobbing, there's plumb-bobby introduced. there's a sweet spot, we're told there's a sweet spot: you hold a club up like this, get a bop, you get a bop bop bop like this this flat flat sway, this bip bip bop. there it is, there it is. there's a sweet spot. you find it and you mark it to remember it, you remember it. there it is. the spot, that's the sweet, the sweet spot.

there's three basic planes. there's a floor, there's a wall, and there's an inclined roof. three basic. there's a wrist-cock. there's wrist cock. I love a game of fly-fishing! I love to go fly-fishing! I've never, I've never been fly-fishing before. I like to think about fly-fishing, about wading about wade in the wade in the wade in the water. we're talking thinking about, well, I am riffing up here a bit. this com puter age, this trigger this trigger of mine, this Meeting Time. the sound of this bell that I am hearing or heard or have heard in moments. they choose you. they chose me.

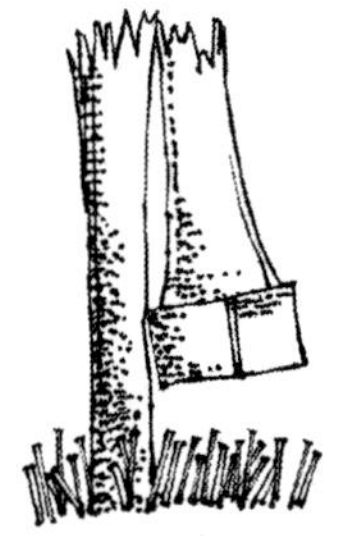

2.

there's a tradition of players playing, there's a tradition, players I am sure you're familiar with say Sam Snead perhaps, Mildred Ella Didrickson Zaharias, Babe perhaps Sergio Garcia, Michelle McGann, Ben Hogan, these players, players like these. there's a tradition of them consulting, I'm telling you, consulting they were consulting with power animals, spirit guides, spirit animals, powerful spirit animal guides offering consultation, consultation, consultation on the course on the course, whereas the caddies of course are trained, learning and training, have learned, the caddies are learning and listening certainly, they listen they have listened they have been listening, caddies and players together always listening to and learning from what these what these what these spirit animals allowed, listening to what the spirit animals offered.

there will have been a day for all these players, this is tired, very much tired of walking, of playing and thinking, thinking about less while accomplishing so much more, so much thinking about concentration, a tradition, a body breaking down into the mind, we find these power guides these spirit animals telling, sounding, advising, consulting, helping caddies helping players by telling what's told. the caddies tell what's told, call it a translation, call it a process of heaving, of unpacking. caddies helping to translate to to to understand what's been allowed, been offered, what is being said, been said, been sounded out. the trick here the trick here the trick here is that nobody is talking about this this hearing, this helping. no one is talking about these relationships, no one is talking this up, no one is up and talking about these spirit animals.

they offer physical support and emotional support, these spirit animals. they offer meta-emotional, truly transitional, call it spiritual support. it is time to Listen Up! now tiger woods, tiger woods, born Eldrick Woods, I think Eldrick Woods, not Eldridge. there is a tradition of nicknames, well tiger by now has actually formally changed his name to tiger, so this is tricky for tiger, because this is no longer a nickname, so it's it's not a good example, no good as a zamp zamp so now just wait now before we carry on like all this gets carried gets so carried away now there's there's a tradition of nicknames, and I want you to understand, this is crucial.

I want you to understand that the actual animals who present, perhaps ongoing, who presented themselves over and over to these players, they do not correlate necessarily, there's no correlation, no way, not necessarily, in no way do the nicknames these public nicknames do not help you guess, you know they are not indica, are not indica-tivated in an individua, the nicka individ indictavidual these nicknames are not indiviz, these are not dicative, are not dicative divs divisible, they don't derive, it's dicative really they aren't indicative indicative. see here how tiger, now woods, call him tiger, works with a rabbit, a plain brown rabbit.

Severiano Ballesteros? back in the mid eighties late eighties you could see him on TV, you could see Seve in those moments, those moments of deep thinking, call it thought. he was consulting with a snapper, the sharp nose sharpie, a snapping, a pointy, pointed, a snapping, it was a snapping turtle. you know I'm sure, I'm sure Seve, he must have freaked, just freaked when introduced when introduced at first but then that's what you get. that's what you get. you get. you get what you get. they choose you, they do.

Shhhh. Shh. I think, is that? I think I hear a bird, a bird, a bird in the bush.

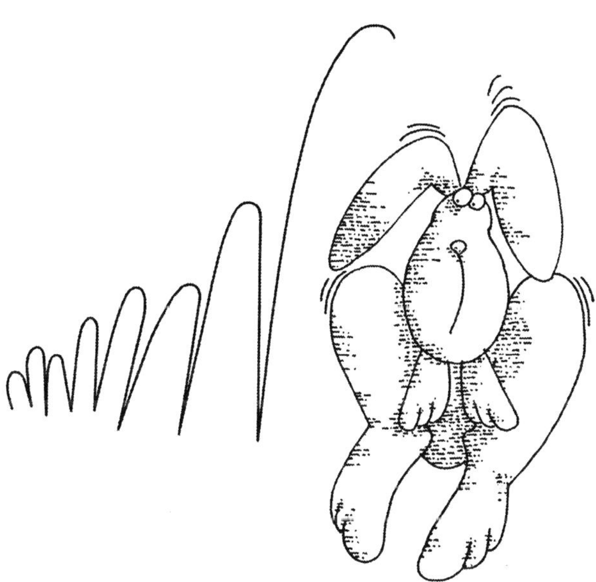

you could see it on TV, on television. there's a tangible presence. a palpa palpa palpability, this deep thinking he would you know he would, when Seve was hot, you could see it. you could see him consulting in the thick of it. he was hot thinking. it was one of those pointy-headed snapper turtles with the head so big it can't fit, actually can't fit its head back in, back into its own shell they say. in the thick of it. he was hot thinking heavy.

Shhh. Shh. I do, I think I do it's there, it's here. I hear it.

crossing across from nine to ten walking from the seventh nine to the eighth nine up and onto the tenth tee, I'm up on the tenth tee. it's a tall tee. I tee the ball up, teed it high, so as to let it fly and I'm gonna hit a high, it's it's it's it's a five par, long and snaky fairway with a bendy kind of way, kind of coming out of a chute. I plan, you want to plan to hit it high left and then there's a creek, you want to keep it left of the creek, take the creek out of play. I hope to hit a good drive, a big high drive slightly drawing, and then I'd have a four iron, like a four iron across the creek for position, need to position my layup I would right there, would hit a four iron right there across the creek leaving me a full pitch, strong pitch like a sharp little punchy pitch to go go go go sixty-five or seventy-five yards to up onto the green, or sand wedge I would hit, I would be planning, I'd be planning it out.

there are many things we might be thinking about. there's the wind, there's the wind blowing, or is it blown? or is it blowing? there's the wind, windy. we feel it and wonder, does it blow itself? some conditions to consider, there are always some conditions. is it wet? is it dry? or was it wet now dry? there's the wind. there's the ground. where's the ground? you know the ground, you must consider the conditions of the ground, this tee box right to left. consider the surface, the feeling, the surface feeling. maybe coming off of the eighth green, we might be smart enough, might have been smart enough to have, as we walked up onto the ninth tee, one hole earlier, we might have been smart enough to notice, we were smart enough to notice, to look, to see, to look over to the tenth green to see where the pin, to see where it's positioned, to see where the pin is positioned, but oh please, my goodness! you remember of course since this is my, remember this is my fourth time round, I am, I am well familiar, well acquainted with where the pin is located on the tenth green on this day walking to the ninth tee off the eighth green, and we're thinking about what else? we're thinking about the shot and the ball and the swing and our feet and you know we're teeing the ball up, we're teeing the ball up and we're visualizing the shot. we see it, try to see the ball in the air, I would imagine, yes this is good, yes.

I would hope to hit a good drive you know, hit a good approach shot, a lay up shot over the creek, imagining this and then that this succession of shots, the success of the shots. you maybe know, remember since I know you know I know that the pin is positioned in the lower quadrant indeed, there it is.

I would hit it crisp, I would decide to hope to hit, that's it, imagine deciding to hope, I do. I hope to hit a crisp three-quarter sand wedge into the middle of the green, and I hope to suck it back, hope to suck it back, hope to suck it back a bit, suck it back a bit. I suck it back a bit. I hope to suck it back, hope to suck it back a bit.

little did I know, I was told outright, the meaning clan hired me as a cleaning man, so just so little did I know like little just so little, I was crossing over now, crossing I'm, I'm, I am exhausted, walking now just walking and playing, playing very well. I was playing very well, and I could see how the lights the lights were lower lower, please lower the lights, and I was playing so well I just kept making the turn you know, but man and woman, that second eighteen stuck out, it was a really good eighteen. I finished up my cheesy toast during that eighteen, little did I know, little did I know like little just little did I know when I was crossing, just crossing, I came to see and to hear how now they are free to choose us, free to choose me, choose you, choose us. they choose. their choice.

they're coming around, coming around, they're coming around in these crucial moments, these crucial moments when needed, they're needed as we're needing to be guided through time, these moments when wisdom their wisdom is needed when we need wisdom and where we might be lost and we need be found, need be found. out of our minds, we're found out of our minds, maybe out of where where we're, we are where we're out of it, I was out of it. we may be where my mind, our minds, my mind might need be stuffed back in, I needed some stuffing back in.

where was I crossing? I was coming out crossing I am crossing across, walking now I notice that the halfway house is closed. that's OK. it was open earlier. I noticed it had closed down, but now if it had been, if it had been open, I might have got a tuna, gotten myself a tuna sandwich you know a tuna fish salad sandwich with a very crisp, I would ask for a tuna sandwich with very crisp very cold celery. there's a woman in there that makes her tuna salad with a lot of raw red onion, and I don't care for that so much, so I would probably have asked for a grilled cheese if she'd been in there, but since I had had, since I had had so much cheesy toast earlier during the round, filled up, just Full Up! I would definitely have gotten a soda, a cola with ice, that ice, these beautifully bored-out cylindrical-like nub nub, very nubby round nubs, very round ice nubs like rabbit poop, no like petting zoo farm feed shaped ice, like pellets, it's like frozen ice pellets, very crunchy that ice is cold it is.

where is it? where is it? who's that? I want to go back, I want to go back to the LPGA, the senior tour before they were the champions or the masters or whatever they call them now. I want to go back to banter, to the banter round the place where, there's a place where the players playing, I mean really playing, well the place where they need to be is winning golf tournaments, and that is what the power animals are here to help them do ongoing, charged with doing for them, doing this for them, willing and able. these guides, you know and again you know Jack Nicklaus, the Golden Bear, ha! he's nicknamed as such so you know just so, the Golden Bear, what do you think he was getting advice from? huh? a Golden Bear? is that right? the Great White Shark, huh? what do you think, do you think there's a shark out there? now, back to Jack, no Greg.

now in Greg Norman's autobiography he admits, he admits to be in, to be in hoots, cahoots, colluding, in his autobiography: *Normal Norman*, he admits he was presented with his power animal, his animal guide, Greg's animal guide was an alpaca, a long neck soft hair. now Norman, no, back to Jack, now Jack Nicklaus Jack Nicklaus, Jack Nicklaus, Nicklaus is from Ohio. perhaps they have bears in Ohio, maybe, I mean you know surely you know how big a guy he was back in the day, he was a big guy and he had blonde hair so someone came round to calling him a Golden Bear one day one might think, I might think, now you might think, just tossing this out I guess, maybe they have bears in Ohio, maybe they even have Golden Bears in Ohio. I am just trying to demonstrate say demonstrate simply indicate to you that the nicknames are not reliable, now this is crucial, let me go on. where they need to be, the place where these players need to be, you ask, "where do they need to be?"

they need to be winning golf tournaments. these players need to be making the good decisions. they're listening as they're presented, caddies included, listening as they're presented with these power animals. I have a sneaking merely a sneaky if not sneaking suspicion, speculative perhaps yet sound yet sneaking, Jack, back to Jack, he was in consultation with a wood duck, get me, a beautiful wood duck, Festival Wise! now in Jack Nicklaus's autobiography: *my way or the*, it's *my way or up your your highway, my way is up your high way on the way, I'm on my way up your*, no? *I'm in the way, I'm on the way*, wait, no. *make way? I'm on the way Up Up your highway?* in Jack Nicklaus's autobi ography, *my way or the*, it's *my way up your your highway, my way is make way*, no. it's *My Way Heading on Up the Highway*, or no, it's in his autobiography, he devotes an entire chapter to the, to the the, to the Golden Bear, to the idea of the conversation being proper, with a proper bear, a golden one. he's trying to get us to hear it, to believe it, that he's speaking to his very own golden bear all this time.

Patty Berg, now Patty Berg, now she's my favorite golfer. Patty Berg, now she's a classy lady, you know Patty Berg, she wrote in her autobiography oh Patty oh Patty Berg, in Patty Berg's autobiography: *Patty Berg Burger Patty Burger Berg, do you want fries with that?* Patty? Patty, now in her, in her autobiography: *Patty Berger Burger Berg, do you want cheese on that?* she wrote, you remember who she is, yes she's the one who would turn, she'd turn her visor over, pull it over to the left if she wanted to hook the shot you know or she would reach up and yank her visor to the right, turn her visor over to the right if she wanted to cut the shot, fade it, or you know she'd flip the visor up over upside down on her head if she was needing to hit a big big tall shot up and over, or I think she might even, she was she might even've pushed her visor down low if she wanted to you know carve out a little punch shot, hit it low like so, well in her, she wrote in her autobiography

Patty Berg Patty Berg admits that she was presented with, consulted with a spirit animal and that animal that guide was a pit bull, a big wide headed pit bull with big shovel jaw, big shovel jaw pit bull maw maw, big pink red maw maw maw.

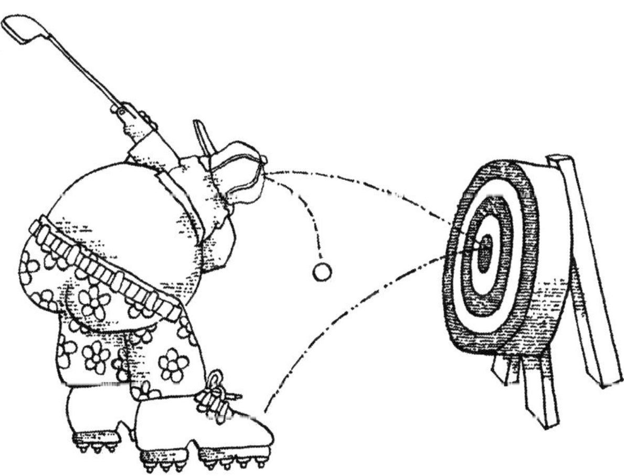

3.

there's a guy.

there's a guy, and there's a guy from Puerto Rico you know, Chi Chi Rodriguez. you got there Patty Berg Pit Bull, hear it there, well Chi Chi coincidentally sounding much like the ear with the ear sounding what it sounds like Patty Berg Pit Bull, noticing Chi Chi and his real world spirit animal is you know Chi Chi Rodriguez you know his real world spirit animal, his real world animal guide? well you know generally they are common animals, but Chi Chi in Chi Chi's situation, his guide is small, a marsupial, a small marsupial, a very small marsupial, a very small Japanese marsupial, the very small Japanese marsupial: MonChiChi. you hear it there? you hear it hit like it does? and the action, his action? oh well Chi Chi's action is legendary, so well I know you're familiar, must be familiar with the sword play on the greens, yes? legendary, this sword play. he makes a putt and then he flips the club head over, and he's holding the shaft really, grasping just above, grasping on the hosel. there he is using the grip as a sword point just showboating, my goodness knows he's showboating bold as can be, but you know back in eighty-seven, eighty-six maybe, 1986, I bet Chi Chi won maybe nine, ten events on the Senior Tour and he flips the club over, makes a putt and he's showboating, and he's, you know what he's doing? he's acting, he's acting like he's slaying a dragon or something, fighting something, sword-fighting something fire-breathing. that's what he's doing, but is that what he's doing? he's stabbing. he's stabbing at the hole like stabbing at something dancing, he's dancing around making putts like, like what? like he's a matador! a Puerto Rican matador making putts, I guess so, but believe me tell you right here, it was not about the putts, no. it's not about the putting, the sword-fighting is not, the sword-fighting's not about the putting alone, the thing is, the thing is, it's about the animal, the MonChiChi, it's about the MonChiChi, it's about the power animals as they do overflow they do tend to flow over, the voice ever-present in your head perhaps, it is the advice forthcoming and sometimes this advice you know it's flowing over here like this flow might go strong: take it back farther, take it back farther, Chi Chi, take it back farther, get it to parallel, Chi Chi, get it back to parallel, Chi Chi, come on, get it back to parallel, come on get it back get it back get it back get it back, take it back farther, take it back farther, look unto young Daley the orangutan hitting heels at the top, get it back to parallel at least back to parallel, come on Chi Chi, you're leaking power at the top Chi Chi, take it back farther, take it back farther, Chi Chi, take it back farther, get it to parallel Chi Chi get it back to parallel, faster to finish, faster to finish, don't de-cel, don't de-cel, fast through to finish Chi Chi, fast to finish, slow back fast through, slow back fast through, slow back fast through, Chi Chi. well, it might go like that and he spins the club around where the grip itself is the sword point, you would think as everyone thought, you would think as everyone did, it was legendary showmanship, call it showboatsmanship, you know he he he makes a putt, and he's trying to intimidate

as he's stabbing he's stabbing he's stabbing his opponent, no! he's swatting. if you look at the footage, at the films of him playing in his prime, if you look at him during regular play, during the rounds, he's swatting constantly, every hole, walking down the fairway, he's swatting, swatting right swatting left always doing this sword thing. what's he doing? he's swatting at the MonChiChi. they're mobbing him globbing like glomming onto him just aflooding him with this overflow might go: take it back farther, take it back farther, Chi Chi, take it back farther, get it to parallel Chi Chi, at least parallel, get it back to parallel. well, no! he refused, he refused, he stayed so quick, so short, just plain refused to take it back farther, he refused to take it back any farther, even after even after he goes and gets his face stretched I think, you know, I mean his face, have you seen his face? my gawd, his poor face, it's like beautiful like stretched melted plastic is so beautiful, oh gawd I can't, I just can't, can you? have you thought? do you? do you think?

woah, there's a finch in here.

Nancy Lopez, prairie dog. Tom Kite, screech owl. as I think of these, just think as I think of these players' names and corresponding spirit animals, I'll mention them, just call them out, I will tell now my knowledge, I know it's piling up on you, but easy goes it, they say they say steady wins it, follow me here, stay with me here now, Tom Kite was corresponding, consulting if you will, he was involved with a screech owl, fully speaking and telling, showing and speaking and telling, you know I do wonder what I wonder is what might, what exactly might that owl? what did that owl allowl?

you have someone like Craig Stadler, Craig Stadler and this is where my idea or go on and call it a theory, this is where my theory about the player nicknames, about how the nicknames, ha! you're seeing how the common nicknames don't help you understand, actually this, this one instance with Stadler is where my theory breaks down here right here because Craig Stadler, known as the walrus, The Walrus! he was known to be in fact, in fact presented with just that, a walrus. see where I'm going here? in his autobiography, and this is a guy, understand me here, this is a guy who is all about all about the power package you know, the assembly point, the envelope, the power package assembly point and the loading action, the delivery path, the envelope, the power package assembly

point delivery path. Stadler is a guy, this is a guy who is all about the power package and the envelope. Stadler is all about his knee action and lag loading, left wrist action lag loading knee action lag loading left wrist action knee action lag loading, left wrist action lag loading knee action lag loading left wrist action lag loading. in his autobiography he admits to taking advice from, to being consulted through all his years traveling on tour, consulted by a walrus, in fact he goes on and blames the walrus for the decision to put the towel down, he put that towel down up under that tree to keep his knees from getting wet, the walrus! got two strokes, he blames the walrus! eventually eventually eventually if you do go ahead and finish, if you did finish the autobiography, if you did, if you did, it's Craig's, let's see Craig's autobiography was, it's titled *Ladies*, no, it's *Ladies*, no *Girls Girls*, no now come on, it's, it's in the book Craig's autobiography, it's something with, is it? it's just Craig, right? no no, it's Craig: *hurry along with me and*, it's Craig: *hurry along with me and I'll tell you about my life, I'll tell you about my life*, no it's Craig, it's *Craig Craig*, it's *Craig: come along and skip*, no it's *come along and skip with me and skip*, no, *walk with me*, what? it's *skipping* no *walking* or *walk with me*, no no, it's Craig, it's titled Craig Stadler's autobiography is *Craig: skip skip along with me and we can chat about my life*, I think that's the subtitle maybe, but no matter. he's talking, he's talking in the end about the breakup, he talks about the spirit walrus leaving him, just awful, so despondent, you know when they quit you, oh! when they quit you, oh well.

back to Jack, clearly I have done a lot of research, so back to Jack, if you look at the films at the footage, and really look, really focus on him, you will always, always see him seemingly reconnect, you see him, he finds it, you see him reconnect, his Meeting Time always happening near the small ponds. it's a re-composition, he's de-composing himself near the water, near the small ponds, and then building up, rewriting from within what is offered up from without and this is going way back, we're talking about the big white hair, seeing, if you look on the films, seeing Angelo, late sixties early seventies, Angelo crouching and hearing, always crouching and hearing wise words whistled in the wet, and Jack is all ears too, down low by the reedy ponds, and my read on this is crucial. OK, he's down near the reeds. I see it like this, and you could get me here, I see it. spirit bears, of course spirit bears, spirit golden bears do need to drink, they do. they need water surely, so you could, if you were to really look close. OK, if it were to really be a bear, a spirit bear, that's where we're still at believe it or not, it would not be completely implausible that it be near the small ponds where they may meet, since spirit bears may need drink, but I have suspicions sneaking up, concerns unfounded but grounded in rather hefty research, that it was a beautiful wood duck as consort to Nicklaus, helping him get where he needed to be, namely winning golf tournaments, a wood duck helped him get to be winning major golf tournaments. oh the litany, the litany, it was the tedious litany which proved so powerful: watch the elbow, you're flying the elbow, Jack, you're flying the elbow, watch the elbow at the top, Jack, watch your elbow watch your elbow.

that's the quality, profound yet airy, there it is. this is the kind of stuff, top notch stuff you're getting from these spirit guides at this level, at this top level, vital, crucial. call it crucial advice. call it significant. call it quality. sometimes you fix, you fix on something good, something quality. Medium Cadet.

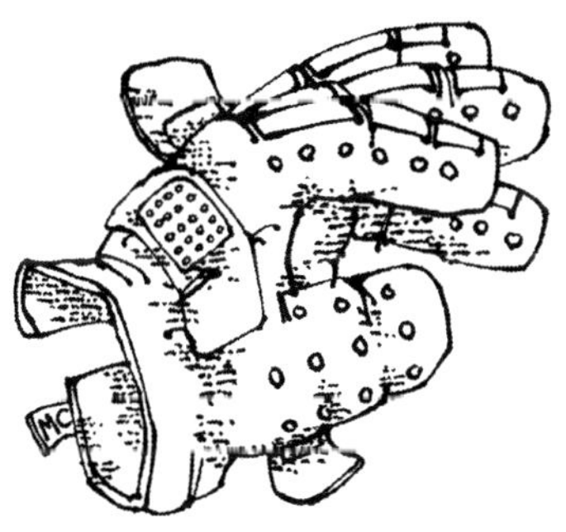

we've got Fuzzy Zoeller, Fuzzy Zoeller Fuzzy Zoeller wasn't fuzzy was he? Fuzzy was fuzzy, and then his wife from the wings his wife his wife runs in whispering, "Fuzzy WAS fuzzy he was he was."You got Fuzzy Zoeller you know his spirit animal, a tarpon, sleek and wet. Fuzzy Zoeller wasn't fuzzy was he? Fuzzy was fuzzy, and then from the wings his wife his wife runs in whispering, "Fuzzy WAS fuzzy he was he was."

Nick Faldo, a fox, reddish-brown. Michelle McGann, a strong-legged ostrich. Paul Azinger, a river otter. you can see it in his neck, in his mullet, Paul Azinger, a river otter. Phil Mickelson, an octopus.

now I love me some Mickelson, ha, I remember you know, octopus. I remember the shot, I do remember seeing him play in college, footage of Mickelson, call them highlights. Mickelson, an octopus. he had hit, he did hit a shot over the green, skipped it over the green, the ball ran through the back bunker, straight through it, across the bunker up behind the green and it came to rest in the rough slanting down, it's slanting down back toward the hole, resting up on the down, up on the downslope of the grass beyond, so this is the shot, here's the pin, this is the shot, this is the shot, funny stance true but this is the shot, here's the pin, here's the pin, this is the shot right here, and what does Mickelson do? granted, he's left-handed so bear with me here, but what does he do? Mickelson, an octopus, the octopus? well, he aims away, aims away, aims away from the pin and just scoops it, scoops it up and over his head, well he can't scoop it, no, you can't scoop the ball, you're actually not permitted to scoop the thing, but he flips it, flips it up, flicks it up and over, properly struck but launched straight up and over his head behind, over his head behind and onto the dancefloor and he parks it, stops it before the hole, see? flips it up backwards and stops it before the hole, huh? what just happened? how is it even real? Mickelson, an octopus. Anika, Anika Sorenstam, a hawk.

Orville Moody, also known as The Sarge (spelled with an "a" I think it is, even though sergeant is spelled sergeant, somehow sarge is spelled Sarge, probably for purposes of easy sounding, easy seeing and easy sounding, much like the choice one might make to spell hosel hozzle, now returning) Orville Moody, also known as The Sarge, a yak, but a very fast walking yak. in his autobiography, now he's known, there's no no no denying, there's no no no one denying, trust me that no one would be denying that Orville Moody was a very fast player, the Sarge, you've read his autobiography? you've read it? the Sarge? *Orville Moody: the Sarge in Charge*, in his autobiography, you've read it? he talks about how fast that yak had to be, in fact he describes that yak as remarkably fast, in fact remarking on how fast the yak was as a walker, and he talks, he goes on to discuss how the yak initially got him into the long putter, definitely one of the first spirit guides to go long with the putter. Moody made it work, he made the long putter work for him and his fast ass.

These relationships last a lifetime. my first Meeting Time was long long ago and my guide, my power animal guide, and this is where for me, you know this relationship for me, this is where for me, oh I do, I just love the chance to share this with you. this relationship, my relationship with the spirit animal, this is where for me, my guide, this is where for me, my guide is in fact guideS! plural. hear the difference? I have a trio. it's subtle, but indeed, they chose me. one, two, three. they chose me and of the three, not one, no single member of them three has risen to the FORE! ha, you know I joke jokes but this is serious here.

I haven't played the game in years, but I recall they were harmonious, might say a harmonious threesome I might, but now I haven't heard from them in many years, three years by my count of years.

I have not been playing, simply have not been playing the game, and just since coming into this space this performance place you know, since I started thinking about what about what it is I am telling you, what I am telling you right now, I am thinking about what I am telling you right now, yes since I have been hitting a lot of golf shots in here, hitting lots of shots up against the wall, against this netting, hitting shots up into that shit up there, and I hit a few shots over that way, bounced a few shots off the door. I hit a couple hundred five irons into these here, what are

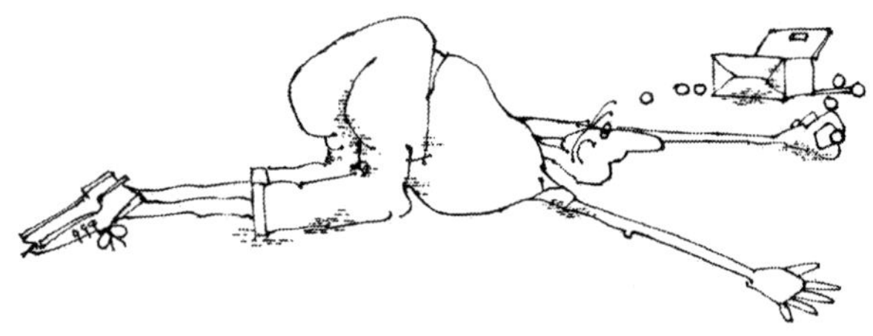

these? what is this? these are curtains could be yes, they are called curtains I could call them. having been in here and starting the juice to flow, new juice flowing and thinking starting to think about this stuff, old times, starting to think about this stuff, old times and new, starting to hit some shots, warming myself up a bit and there it is, they're back! they've come back to me after all these years, I just, well, we're back, right back where we left off. they know me like they do, they know me like it is nobody's business, they've got me pegged. they've got, they've got more stickers, more stickers on me than you can shake a sticky sticker at, and when I was, when I was where I was, you asked, what was the question? you asked me where I was? you asked me where was I when I first met my trio, you asked? well, I will tell, I will.

well, I was back on the tenth tee, I was eleven years old on the tenth tee. eleven years old on the tenth tee. on the tenth tee, I chose my driver. I teed the ball up tall. I was crossing over, walking I was, crossing over from from nine to ten, crossing over from my seventh from my seventh round of nine to my to my eighth round to my eighth round of nine, walking up onto the tenth tee, I heard a bell. I heard a bell. this was, this was my Meeting Time, and and you know maybe in your home you have a dinner bell, I do. I heard a bell, the bell the bell, very same I spoke of earlier, a sound bell.

let me, I should first, to explain that this is real, see. let me explain the difference because for me it actually does, it actually does, there actually is a bell, my trio. there it is. see what you see what what I'm concerned with what, what concerns me more than anything is that that there is this, you see my trio, my trio, now there's my my ponypuppykitty, when I first met my ponypuppykitty, it came along with all of this, all of this apparatus, this this buggy with wheels and a seat like a bench and fenders and a yoke kind of thing that comes out to grab and fasten up on top, up on top straddling, like a belt, not a saddle, it's kind of a harness type mid-section garter-like garter middle garter garter thing that goes round the pony, it goes round the pony's middle, and then near the puppy and kitty, on their level, we find a bell, there's a bell up on top, there it is it is mounted on top, right there, up on top there's a bell.

there is a bell, and this bell, you have to find it, this sounding of a ringing, it is seen, but we need first to find it, you you need to find it, you need to find it with your mind, find it, find it with your mind, it being whatever you lost, and when I am really playing well, striking and rolling and scoring well, I can seemingly I can I can I can find them, I can find the bell. first the bell comes, it comes in the air, see I cannot summon the bell, cannot summon it out of the thin, but I can well I can I can find the bell, I can find the bell, find it with my mind, find it with your mind, I do. you should. I have. we could have such an ability, seemingly find them, I can find them in my mind.

(((sound: bell noise, rolling gadinkga dink gadinkga dink))) do you remember, member? do you member member? well I already, well I have never, have you ever? obviously I might mention the meaning clan fired me as their cleaning man. here it comes, they do.

4.

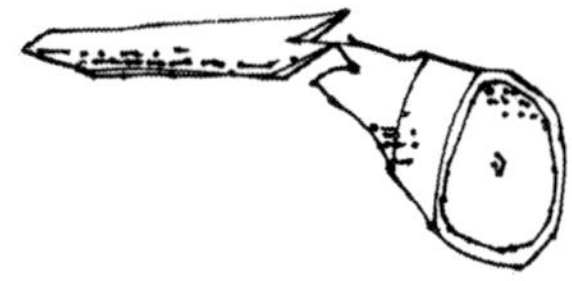

these are very nervous creatures as they have very, very bad eyesight, well at least my pony does. can't really, I can't exactly speak for the puppy or the kitty since they just, they just sit there in the buggy. I haven't exactly seen them out and about, they just seem to stay seated, to stay in their seats on the buggy, the bench on the buggy. they sit.

pony says nneee, glory and honor! pony says nneee, glory and honor! pony says, and I hear in its breath this micro this miniature this micro mini noise of nature, a natural noise I hear when I listen, I listen carefully listen closely I hear in its breath, I hear it softly, I hear it so sweetly, ah go spell: what kind of shoes are you gonna wear? golden slippers, and what kind of robe are you gonna wear? long white robe. golden slippers I am bound to wear when I reach my hebenly home, golden slippers I am bound to wear when I reach my home. oh yes yes yes my lawd, I'm gwon jine de hebenly kweyerr, yes yes yes my lawd, when I reach my home.

what is beyond the nneee? there it is. pony says nneee, glory and honor! there are funda, fundamentals. there's a general frowning on these these fundamentals, but I hear, I hear them there closely whispered: feet feet, two feet a foot apart, two feet shoulder width, two feet there they are, maybe a bit broader than shoulder width wide, two feet a foot apart, two feet a big foot apart, two feet there they are. pony says nneee, gathering strength, glory and honor! back foot is perpen, pretty much perpendicular to the target, you choose a target here, choose a target, and then right here, see? see the target?

make the T, there it is. make the T, there it is. two feet a foot apart, back foot perpendicular to your target, choose a target, make a T, that's where your back foot should be. stand behind, pick a mark, stand behind, pick a mark and connect dots, connect dots, ball to mark, mark to target, get it? connect and see, connect and see it happening, it is happening now, you stand behind, you pick a mark, now please understand how you must, you must picture the shape of the shot, picture the shape of the shot, picture the shape of the shot, picture the shape of the shot, go go go go!

pony says nneee, knees bend, knees bend inward, weight, now weight is central, centralish, an athletic ready, an athletic ready stance, an athletic ready stance. I am ready I am ready athletic, I am ready, my stance is an athletic ready stance. your knees bend, my knees bend inward, bend them inward as if holding but not juicing a large Florida grapefruit.

arms, arms, left arm and a right arm, there they are. left arm, if it is the front arm, assuming northpaw pref, right foot trailing, there it is. left arm, the left arm is tall and straight, straightish. right arm say right elbow tries to tries to get to push the button in your belly, yes elbow, the right elbow, what am I gonna do? what am I gonna do? what am I gonna try to do with the right? where's your belly? where's your belly? show me your belly. where's your, where's your belly? where's your bellybutton? where's your bellybutton? come here. where's your bellybutton? OK. right elbow now, the right elbow now tries to go in to touch to touch to touch your navel, to touch your navel, that's it, there it is. right there ah! ah! right there ah! right there ah! ah! right there ah! right there ah! ah! right there ah!

(((sound: elbow navel noise goes poing bip poing bip)))

and then the knees, hold it. the weight is not in the toes, not in the heels, might be slightly back in the heels, but not all the way, never all the way. take an athletic ready stance, feel it in the insteps, the weight is in the insteps, now prep to coil coil coil. prepare to coil, can we participate? preparing to rev it up, revving it up. OK. can I get a finger up to watch, a finger up to watch for my head moving back? it helps, you want a stationary head, not up, not down, not back. I have pictures of myself playing when I was twelve and I'm hitting the ball and my head is like this like this like a tray you could serve a beer on my ear, so put your finger up, we're participating please, now check it out, is my head moving back? is my head moving back? is my head moving back?

oh! watch out, there's a finch.

so so so so so, step though to finish through the ball see the weight move through the ball, the weight moves through the ball, so step through and step through, now don't step through and point, there it is. point the toe, now pick up the foot, there it is. the weight transfers.

shoulders back, bend from the hips not the waist. chin up, chin up, keep your chin up, your chest full, shoulders back, bend from the hips not the waist, right elbow right elbow right elbow.

you'll hear "keep your head down." you'll hear you must keep your head down, and you will hear, "eyes on the ball, keep your head down." so when you hear "keep your head down" and you do keep your head down, know what you get? want to know know what you get? you get no room, no room, right here. no room, no room for your shoulder to turn, you get no room for your shoulder to turn, there's no room for your shoulder turn, for a full shoulder turn. so, keep your head down? no! right here, no room, no room for your shoulder to turn, right here, no room, no room for your shoulder to turn. no room right here. so, keep your head down? no! right here, right here, no room for your shoulder to turn. OK. chin up, in general, we need chin up, not head down, shoulders can turn to tuck up under the chin, left shoulder cap rolls under chin, there it is. we go go go go go go. my slow pony says nneee, now back foot is perpendicular to your target. that's it, pick a target, make a T, that's where your back foot should be. do like this. right hand makes, watch the,

see if the right hand is here at the perpendicular and the left hand, say if the fingertips are trying to, see them point out here, fingertips point for the target such that, see here? see the T, the T like this with the hands? like this. like this, see? see here? yes. back to where we start, we started. OK, we're starting!

we're starting now! feet, knees, hips hips hips, navel, chest, shoulders, chin up, eyes down, right elbow, right elbow, left hand, left arm, and go spell: keep your quack trimmed and keep your, position one, platform. quack QUACK platform. quack platform. quack platform rod, rod and claw, position one, position two, bring a torch Jeanette Isabella, position two, position two, stick it out, like a pregnant, like a quack, position two, stick it out, cute duck sticks out too much, position two, position three to the top, come hurry and run, bring a torch, come hurry and position three, Isabella position three to the top, position four position four position four and a half, quack, feet feet quack feet knees hips right elbow left hand left arm position four and a half, quack position four and a half position four and a half position four and a half position three to the top, position four, position four and a half, position four and a half, come hurry and run, position platform. position five at impact, five at impact, give me five at impact, position five is impact, high impact, impact, right hand right hip, right elbow right elbow left hand left arm, keep your quack trimmed trimmed and burning, keep your position one position one platform rod and claw quack platform quack, come hurry and run. bring a torch Jeanette Isabella, bring a torch at five, position five at impact, five at impact, give me five at impact, position five is impact, high impact, right hand right hip, right elbow right elbow left hand left arm, keep your quack trimmed trimmed and burning, keep it, keep your position drawing nigh, we've started.

we're starting, we're starting now: feet knees hips hips hips navel, chest, shoulders. ah – number two creeping, out creeping out like I said, "it is a very slow pony, slow pony clomp clomp clomp clomp, go the slow pony's clompers. clomp clomp clomp clomp, what's that? here comes a puppy."

(((sound: puppy sound rruff rolll rrr uh uh fuff)))

next one has a bit of a rruff to it, that's the puppy. number two of the trio, my roughneck trio. puppy says rruff, the puppy says rruff, and go spell: puppy says rruff, puppy sezzezekiel saw the wheel, way up in de middle of de air, ezekiel saw de wheel, way in de middle of de air, wheel in a wheel in a wheel in a wheel in a wheel in a wheel in a wheel, puppy sezzezekiel saw the wheel, the puppy this puppy my puppy says rruff, puppy tells me we must deal, spoken, puppy says we have associated planes, we have the floor, we have the door, we have the floor, we have the door, and on the floor we have a mattress, maybe we tip the mattress up, maybe we tip the mattress up to be like the door. we have the floor, and we have the door. we have a mattress on the floor, or we have a mattress like the door, and what if, and maybe we have a mattress in the middle, and when I say middle, I mean forty-five degree mattress. why would it be forty-five degree? why would we have such a thing? a middle mattress? VISUALIZATION – VISUALIZATION.

(((sound: singsong-clippy-noise-flows-cut-and-paste-tastes-of-salt-leaden-doors-of-the-vault-bend-with-age-till-the-cage-cracks-page-boys-bangs-bang-and-flit-in-the-wind-flit-and-re-wind-gin-be-juice-in-and-out-of-the-prot ruding-spout-on-springs-undress-mattress))) puppy says rruff. right hand right hip, right hand right hip, hit the mattress on the forty-five, hit this mattress, right hand right hip right hand right hip, hit the mattress, at position five through the ball, right hand right hip at the ball, through impact. OK. platform, OK. where is your weight? you keep your weight on the ground where it would seem, OK. where is it? we can see it. we can see it is here. it is definitely the ground here to tap, go and tap it. tap it. tap it harder. beat it, gently. beat it, gently. believe it. there it is. believe this is it. this is the ground. this is the ground.

on the ground, the ball rests quietly. The ball rests quietly slowly becoming aware of nothing. there it is, so motionless. it softly rests. does not disturb, does not yell. rarely does it hit you back. it does not oppose you, the ball is a friend. puppy, puppy? puppy says rruff, puppy says rruff. VISUALIZATION.

puppy says VISUALIZATION, like dragging, no. it's like a hanging, like hanging a picture on the wall, driving tacks, it's like driving tacks, like driving tacks, tacks or brads, it's like a hammer, it's like a hammer, like a hammer and a nail, it's like you have a nail and you have a hammer, you hit the nail with the hammer, you hit the nail with the hammer, that's what it's like. no, that's not what it's like, that's not what it's like at all.

what is it then, you ask? it's like clipping, like a clipper, it's like you have a clipper, you have a clipper and a nail, so it's a nail clipper, you have a nail clipper and you clip the edge, the edge of the nail, you clip just the edge of the nail, you clip the nail, the edge of the nail, you clip the nail, it's the clipping, it's like the clipping, it's a clipping, no, that's wrong, it is not, no, no, it's not like that, it's definitely not like that at all.

what is it then? you ask again? it's like it's like you, like you have, like you have, you have fingers and you pinch you pinch you pinch, you're fast, you're fast, you've fast fingers and you are fast pinching, you're pinching fast, you are very fast when you are pinching, it's like you're a fast pincher with fingers. I'm fast, and I'm a pincher. I'm a fast pincher, I pinch so fast, I pinch I'm pinching, I'm pinching so fast, I'm pinching, I'm pinching so fast, I'm a pincher pinching like so fast.

(((sound:fast-pinch flurry goes pinch I pinch I pinch pinch)))

may seem unreal, watch my cartwheel, my floor exercise, I think I may surprise, with my ability, supreme agility, I run vault flip and twist, I am balancing on my weaker wrist, ya! gold medal gymnast me! rruff, gold medal gymnast me! miaow, ha ha hee, ha ha cough cough, ho yo yo ya.

yo kitty. hey kitty, I see number three. there's a kitty, there she is. have you ever met a kitty? have you ever met a kitty, ever met a kitty before? mee me meeow meeow miaow, kitty says miaow, kitty says miaow, kitty says miaow. kitty's interested in the refined articulation of the smaller muscles, she is, those being the hands and fingers and toes those muscles, miaow, she says miaow, she says it is best, plainly put, it's best for you to start out, when you start out, plainly put, best if you if you start, when you do, when you start, you start out trying to be a hooker. it is best for you to start out trying to be a hooker, and we have long since started, she said, clean and clear. it's best if you do not even pretend to be able to find perfect balance. it's not even a possibility, considering all that is ongoing. she says, kitty says "miaow." kitty says "miaow."

kitty says we must concern must concern ourselves exclusively exclusively concern ourselves with hip turn knee action lag loading left wrist action, left wrist action lag loading knee action hip turn hip turn knee action lag loading hip turn hip turn knee action hip turn knee action hip turn pivot, lag loading, pivot, pivot, knee action hip turn and please do not even pretend to be able to find perfect balance, such a thing as perfect balance after you've lost it, have you lost it? as you start out, have you? have you lost it? kitty says miaow to all that, kitty says miaow to me she does. it's best best if you start perfect, hip action, start at the beginning, best to be starting from the beginning trying to be a hooker, lag loading, if you have a mind, a mind to find them here calling, knee action hip turn hip turn, they are sounding out, we're starting. starting at the beginning, best to be starting from the beginning trying to be a hooker, damn it!

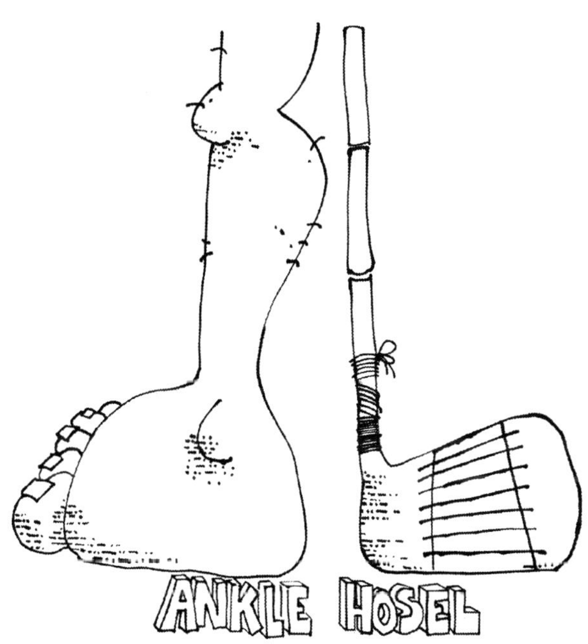

5.

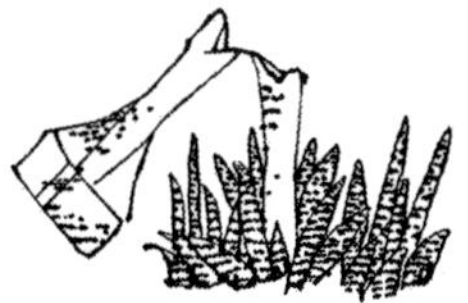

I have a bag here, I have a black bag here, I have a black plastic bag here, I have a black plastic garbage bag here filled with little piggy pigs, little pigs, just little oh little, look herein look, look here at this one here, a little boy pig as big as a football. I have it here. curly tail, little ribbon, little piggy nose, little ribbon tied here round his neck, oh I have it here, it is such a cute pig. I'm going to put him down, I'm going to put him down, I'm going to put him down right here in the way. now what I want you to do, I need you to start, you need to start thinking of turning hands over, forearms rotate, hands turn over and club head, the club head, see it, see it, see it, start thinking about turning those hands over and understand now what it means, what does it mean to be a hooker? pronate to the supine, supinate to the prone like hookers do, like a hooker does it. that might be it. you know all the best ball strikers do it. are you wondering about how to start talking yourself into thinking about becoming a hooker?

now the pig, the pig is right here in the, oh, the piggy? there, piggy! piggy! there you are, ha ha ha hee hee oh you are oh you, kitty says you you pinch a piggy booty, pinch a piggy booty, it's OK, shh, it's OK, it's OK, shh, I know, I know now now I need you to, I need you to start to consider, I'm gonna put him back down, right here, right here in the way. I need you to, OK. kitty says, so kitty says miaow, kitty says miaow, kitty says we need you to start turning your hands over, so set up set up, go on and set up set up set up set up to the ball, set up to the ball, and goodness me, you know oh no, just oh no! where'd you go? piggy! where'd you? OK, there, piggy! OK. calm yourself, it's OK.

now right here, I just want you to, I want you to, set up set up set up, slow routine, see it. first position yourself, address it, set up set up. OK, take it to the top, position three, position three at the top, kitty says take it to the top, take it to the top, that's it. that's it. take it to the top, and go now rotate through to impact and stick it! stick the pig, stick the pig, take it to the top, now start down and rotate wrists through to impact and stick the pig, stick the pig, stick the pig, stick the pig with the toe of the club so hard you have to step on the pig to pull the club head out!

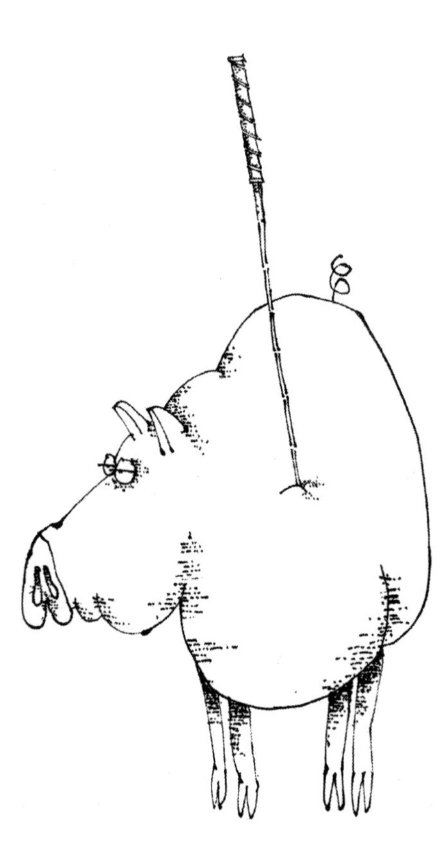

right there. there, there it is. now don't worry, don't worry, don't worry, there's plenty of pigs. he introduced himself as Bobby. now later on, he introduced himself as Bobby now later on, later on I ended up hanging out with the dude. he had black shoes, black socks, huh? he did, ha! he had black shorts, he had black shoes, black socks, black shorts, black belt, black shirt. he introduced himself as Bobby. he had black shoes, black socks, black shorts, black belt, black shirt, black visor, black glove, black tees and these are not tees that he bought black, oh no, no no, these are tees that he painted black. he introduced himself as Bobby. I was hoping this was a statement, a darkness like John Cash or a bladdeladdeladdeladdel purp kind of way like maybe Gary Player had some dark thing to say, but we're waiting, we're waiting, we're waiting, it's a 350 yard, this is just this morning, just this morning, we're waiting on the first tee. it's a 350 yard par four, and he's like well you know he says, "I might I might I just might reach the green." ha! so you know, we're waiting, we're waiting for them to clear off, waiting for them to clear off the green, the group, the group ahead is almost finished, we're waiting for them to clear off the green.

he sets up. we're waiting, he sets up right side of the tee, we're waiting for the group ahead, it's a par four at about three hundred fifty yards in length, and one of the players ahead ahead, his name is massa massa massa massa massa massaire massario massario, I think it's massario, Massario, I think that's the name, there he is and we can see he makes a birdie, he birdies the first hole and now and now and now Bobby knows the guy, this massa massa Massario fella, later on I ended up hanging out, we can see this guy this guy Massario, so Bobby knows the guy, we see him up ahead on the green, he makes this birdie, and he's pumping his arm, pumping his arm and his fist like this, after the putt goes in, there he is on the first hole, first green, he's pumping his fist now, and Bobby now Bobby is pumped now he's pumped he's pumped he's even more pumped, Bobby's miming impact miming miming impact and he sets up on the right side.

he sets up on the right side of the tee and tees it way up on the black tee, look at that black tee, there's a white ball with a black dot, a Spaulding Dot poised and ready, it balances so perfectly, so quietly there up there on that black tee, look at that black tee, I see it, such potential I see it there. look, you look, now Bobby, Bobby is pumped now for all to see he's pumped he's pumped and he's miming impact miming miming impact there, and there is the black tee, white ball, black Dot. he had black shorts, black shoes, black socks, black shorts, black belt, black shirt, black visor, black glove, now takes, he takes his driver, grips the driver, this glossy persimmon, he's miming miming there it is, miming impact, there it is, still and quiet, miming miming with a tall shoulder, tall shoulder, now loosening to wiggle tight waggle waggle hitch up, and to the top... whack!

the ball squirts out low right, the Dot ball hits the fence post, there's a fence and the ball hits it, hits the fence post, see the fence post coming in pretty close, look at that, look at how close that fence comes in, and now glancing after it, following Bobby's ball goes up over our heads, back behind the tee it's sailing so quiet now up and over and back toward the clubhouse.

the ball is behind us, it's back behind the first tee now bouncing onto the patio and there's lots of eyes, lots of people watching while eating while eating breakfast, and there's glass tables and a bumpy rough patio here we go and these and those and there it is, oh no, oh no look at it go, it's bouncing over here over here and it's bouncing over there over here it's bouncing. it hits the wall, and there's coffee, coffee and creamer now spilling and everything everywhere everyone watching, watching the ball bouncing, it bounces itself down into a window well, you know like a window it has like a well, like a well, you know he's looking around quick glancing and shuffling quickly, "oh sorry sorry oh sorry excuse me excuse me sorry sorry." he's over there and he sees he sees he, he sees his, he sees his ball, "there's my ball, I found it, my ball, found it! found it! here it is!" and he's trying, he's not sure thinking, he's looking looks into the window and he pauses, he's peering down into the window, thinking through it, more into it, the window, because now he is down in the well, crawled down with a club, or more hopped down, he hopped into the well and stepped onto the ledge, the sill I suppose, and he's looking, he's pausing, thinking through it, he looks and what does he see?

what does he see? you know you wouldn't normally be looking into this window you know, we're we're on the patio and and would you would you like for me to tell you? totally. would you like for me to tell you, I am going to tell you right now I am telling you what it is he saw in that window right now, he introduced himself as Bobby, later on later on I ended up hanging out with the dude and this is apparently it.

this is apparently what he saw down in it, OK OK what he saw down there in the cartbarn, now underneath. he's looking under the clubhouse now into the cartbarn where we keep the golf carts and the recharger units and the maintenance area, you've been? the buzz, the buzzing batteries and the cobwebs, and the pullcarts, pause. he's pausing looking through down into the maintenance barn cartbarn where they keep the golf bags too, the maintenance area where the crew, the maintenance crew, we have a dozen or so guys and girls on he crew well this crew apparently had been fighting birds, they've been fighting birds, fighting them for years, these chicken roosters fighting roosters, call them cocks, call them whatever now for a while now they've been fighting these birds down under in it and he told me later on cuz I see you know I ended up hanging out, he says he saw he sees, he sees one of the members one of the members of the club named, what was it? it was his name is Franken Franken Frunken, he saw Franken Frunken Frunken back in there, up in there, up under the clubhouse running some, Bobby

saw him, he did see him running some kind of game gambling some pool some gambling crew betting pool, he's making book betting on the birds and it's flying, cash is flying, bills falling folding all palmed and so garr garrulous, this crew, so festive, so fun.

Bobby saw the circle like a pit, he saw it there the pit, there was a short fence surround, like a link, a wire chicken-wire mini-circle spot. now I'm guessing of course as later on you know I asked some questions later, so some of these details are added back in for clear for clearing, but he saw a rooster, one rooster standing. OK. this rooster, this one special chicken rooster on this one special day had been kicking some serious chicken ass, beating all the other birds. mean, he's mean, he's a mean ass rooster, this rooster is totally dominant, completely, he's winning every match on this day today, so Franken Franken Fronken, you know Franken the member had an idea, had coincidentally recently found or saved, sort of found or rescued an owl, an owl, he had he had rescued an injured owl, and so after this rooster had won, been winning all day, well it was in a cage, the owl was in a cage in the cart-barn, nearby, so I had you know it had you know, it had it had feathers, feathery pointy ears, it was a horned owl it was horned with ears with with with pointy feathers for ears, a horned owl, I wouldn't know if it was, if it was a great horned owl, but it certainly was a horned owl and in the cage it was it was very calm a very calm owl, seemed calm in this cage and you know I, I, I got to know the owl earlier in the week. I had I liked the owl, earlier

earlier on I actually got to know the owl, I, I, the owl had been around for awhile you know, a little while, couple of days I guess and I got I got I had gotten to know the owl, earlier I'd hung out with the owl, and it was a nice old girl, lovely really, this owl, our owl. quite unlike really this visiting rooster was mean was mean, it was mean, here just visiting, just brought in, brought in from a different country club to fight and it'd been just destroying all the other rooster chickens.

Bobby said he saw a pile of birds, bodies, he saw bird bodies in a pile, tossed to the side by this visiting rooster, tossed on our turf just killing all the crew's birds and the money, there's the money flying with Franken Franken Frunken following it, see him there hovering and this is you know, he's the member, the member involved decides decided, he was running the pool, the member Franken Franken Fronken decides to, he's thinking big talking fast and says "hello? let's fight the owl!" kind of a grand finale kind of way, a final brawl, let's fight the owl and the idea spreads wide in the dark barn yes, there it is to be, the main event: ah shit! let's fight the owl, you know.

the visiting rooster, this rooster just visiting, came in strutting bad, so let's fight the owl and just see, just to see what might, what might come of it. of course now you know there's a scramble for the money flowing out really flying fast round the pit and they carry the cage into the pen, the pit, the fighting circle and the rooster really looks so mean just spitting hissing like a sick thing, you know this rooster is the meanest old legger, just gonna destroy the owl this old injured owl, you can see it in the eyes, the eyes of the rooster is red, ready to kick the owl's ass, you know I guess they thought, everyone thought, all the crew seemed to be thinking some such and such about the owl's injury, the hurt wing and the rooster being so mean, this rooster chicken knows what it's doing, been killing all day long that's what it's been doing, still stained from the previous fight, what a brawl bathed him red and the pit all sticky red, this rooster is well warmed up, well warmed up, so the member Franken Franken Franken is running the game: "let's fight the owl!" now of course we'll fight the owl, and the rooster is ready and the owl cage is opened and a hush descends soft, the room pauses, but the owl is just standing still, still standing.

6.

they opened the cage, so now they got to poking they poked the owl out into the circle pit and the owl soft steps out with limp talons, her feathery claws get a bit bloody soft stepping out into the sticky red pit, and the men are growling at each other, the whole damn maintenance crew is buzzing, these grasscutters giggling mad, Bobby said, but the owl was still just standing still so quiet so, just so quiet watching like this like this with sleepy owl eyes, slits, just peeking so, and the boy rooster is up up swarming and hissing spitting something, and the owl and the rooster and the men watching clenching jaws and fists and eyes wide wondering at the owl so still, still so still, and the rooster struts fierce now dancing a lurch, it lurches, and the owl so still, and the owl and the rooster. the owl.

the rooster. what did they do? what did they do? what went down? I'll tell what went, what they did down there, I am telling now what they did, what the owl did, what the owl did, it stood there like, "what did I do? what did I do? what did I do?" the owl is just standing there watching like, "what's this rooster's problem? is there a problem? what's up with this rooster?" and the rooster is over there like wah wah wah wah yuh rah rah rah rah caw caw caw caw caw caw you know doing like this really threatening thing, this rooster thing, this hissing spitting chicken thing, a clawing rooster thing.

course I could, I could here, I could actually show, I'll show you what it looked like here, like this you know, doing like this, and doing this with its legs of course the wings are here and see, so my hands see my hands are really its legs or its feet and claws, right? see here like here, like this, I can do it, I could do a little thing like this fast slashing clawing like rah rah rah yuh caw caw caw wah wah caw caw and over and over and when I do when I do like this, this is when the rooster comes forward into it, and the owl is still standing still not doing a thing just watching just sleepy eyes in the pen sitting calm just sitting, well not really sitting, the owl is there just standing nothing, giving

nothing not even a hoot, but then but then the rooster, it's on, and the rooster jumps bad and rushes it rushes over lurching doing its mean dance now with the rah rah yuh yuh caw caw rah rah caw caw, so now the owl, here it is, the owl just once just once just once, so calm so clean just one pump with both wings, the owl just once just phoo, one pump up with the wings about a foot off the ground, with the wings so smooth, just one pump and pause and kwukwa! like this kwukwa! the owl grabs the rooster by it's neck and bites its head off, done. kwukwa! ripped it off, in mid-jump, hovering so clean and calm, so smooth, it was beautiful, clean off.

she tossed the head to the side while the rooster body thrish thrashes backwards undone, squirts out now done. kwukwa! like this, like this see, just standing still again like, "hoo hoo, who's your daddy now, bitch?" boom! pause, boom! it hit hard, it was wild, oh the crew, can you imagine? it was so wild, just perfect, and to finish, the owl, the owl takes two hops back into the cage, and everyone, every single one in the cartbarn is just agape, abuzz, just WHAT? whaaaaaaa?!? whaaaaaaa? oh my gawd! like whaaaaaa! whaaaaaaat? did you? WHAT? oh my gawd! did you see that? did you see that? did you not just see that happen? that was amazing! that was totally amazing! kwukwa!

now, course the owner of the rooster, that mean old legger who'd been winning all day, of course the owner of this champion chicken rooster, the owner who brought the bird, who had raised the bird, the owner who had made so much money off this bird and probably would have continued to win as he traveled to different fight tournaments at different venues in the tri-state. oh well, the owner of the rooster well just he just crumbled mumbling, and stumbled into the pen gazing down at the mess, down at the last few flops twitching dead, there's a dead chicken, and then what did he do? what did the owner of the rooster do? he spins round with a pistol pulled because he is hot, he's mad, he is pissed, and pulls a pistol not on the club member present, no, not on Franken Fronken, no, he pulls his pistol on the owl, on the owl in the cage, and he spins round now he's trained on the owl, and he moves maybe staggers forward always moving forward with a gun, there it is, plain as day. a handgun.

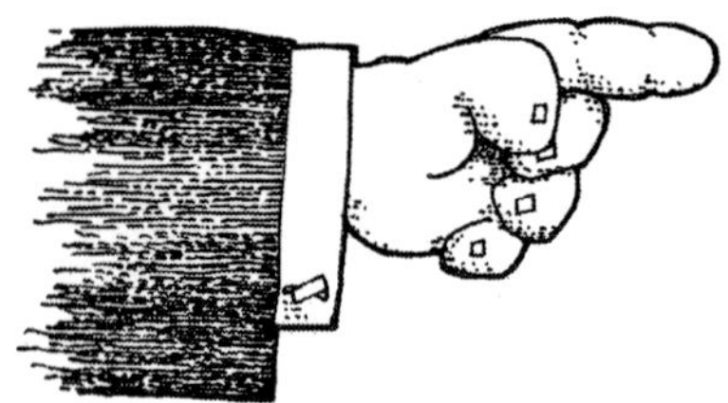

now my father-in-law who told me this story, told how his grandfather was there, no, not his grandfather, it was his father, his father, my father-in-law told me his dad was there so he would be, the father who was there who would be my, let's see, he'd be my grandfather-in-law, so now my, yes he'd be my grandfather-in-law, so he sees this guy pull the pistol on the owl and now you know my grandfather-in-law is really skilled, really quite good with throwing knives and he knows it, so he throws it, he throws a knife and pins the fella's right wrist to the wooden wall of the barn, wabam! however the pistol flips up and falls into the man's other hand and the fella now takes and aims again at the owl, so somehow my grandfather-in-law has another shiv handy, throws and pins his left

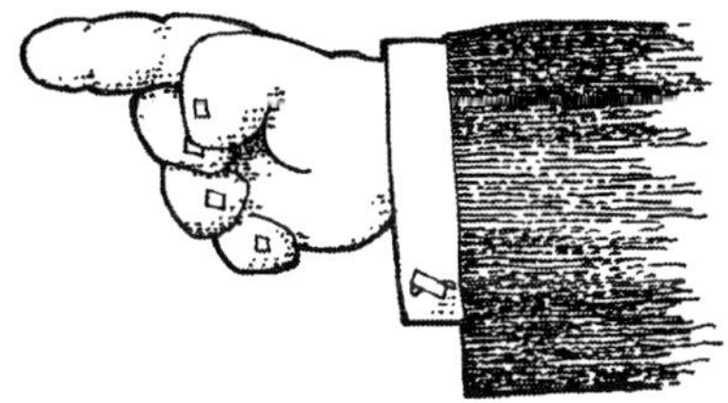

wrist the other wrist to the wall, wabam! there it is against the wooden wall just pinned, just stuck, just caught there both hands, wabam! wabam! in a cross there fixed, and my grandfather-in-law walks right up to the fella, looks him in his eyes and starts right in on his gut, working him over, punching him, punching him in the stomach, "DON'T YOU HURT THAT OWL! DON'T YOU HURT THAT OWL! SHAME! SHAME ON YOU!" working him over, just leaning into him, just wearing his ass out, "SHAME ON YOU! DON'T HURT THE OWL! DON'T HURT THE OWL! DON'T HURT THE OWL!" and that's what Bobby saw in the window.

now back back back, back to the patio, back to the clubhouse patio, to the window well, to the patio with the breakfast on the glass tables, the total disruption. now first off, what do we have here? USGA, there were no markers, no white markers, there never are, right? have you ever? no, there are no markers behind the first tee, so first off, there it is. USGA, do we assume that the area behind the first tee is in fact out of bounds? we thought no, we thought no, so he's playing it, but he needs to drop, so Bobby, now seriously, there it is and it's unplayable. USGA, is it from where the ball lies? does one take two club lengths from first relief or from where the ball lies? the ball's down, you remember it well, way down in the window well. is it from where it lies or from first relief, two club lengths, no closer to the hole, huh? we weren't sure, no rulesbook on hand, certainly no marshals available today, this morning. as we weren't sure, Bobby drops two clubs from where the ball lies, meaning the drop's happening on the rough stone of the patio, bouncing on the patio, so he has to place it eventually because every drop is odd bouncing itself up and left or oddly bouncing right around, so he places it, he places onto the stone patio and see, you know I'm on the tee, I'm on the tee, I'm still on the tee watching and waiting because as far as I'm concerned he's still away.

now he needs to have some furniture moved so I move to help, I'm going back onto the patio to help helping move tables, so we move this and that and there we go, "excuse me here and excuse me there and ok sorry sorry can you just OK thanks here oh sorry sorry about the omelette sorry about the blah blah." OK, move it to this side, and OK he's ready to hit it and he does hit it, he sets up and I think, I think he's gonna chip it, just advance it back into play toward the fairway, but no no he takes a full swing,

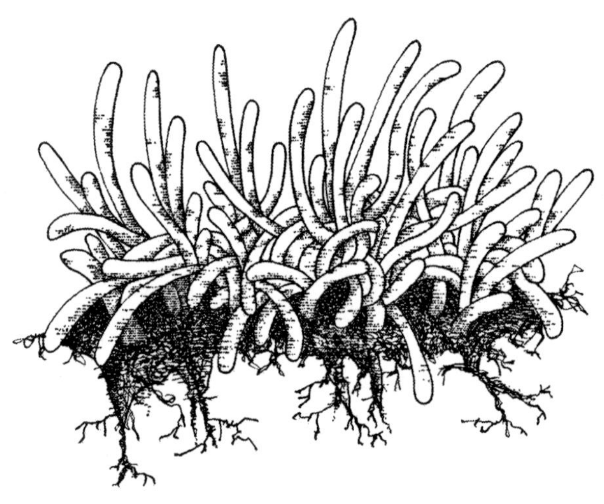

he takes a full swing a big full swing and smacks it. it cracks hard against something solid and bounces up and hits oddly under a table, hits a different table leg, hits this, hits that, hits that again, and oh gawd, it's just awful all ricochet here between this say bip bip bip bip bip and out, it squirts out across the blacktop cartpath.

now he's on the practice putting green, pain in the ass. OK now we all know you know we get relief, we definitely get relief from the practice putting green, don't want people getting up and playing it down, don't want them taking a salmon-size divot out the damn thing. no one wants that shredded up, especially not the greenskeeper, so you know free relief. he drops he does and the drop is gold, soft and beautiful just sitting up all fluff, fluffed up perfect, just perfectly there, look there it is, so good like it's teed up and from the patio we hear, we can hear it real loud, it's really loud and proud: "cantalupé frambuesa cantalupo raspsberries and the fresh snooper soup" or some such something.

now Bobby chooses a driver, same club he was originally hitting, only now he's sitting pretty in the rough alongside the practice putting green, he's there between the cartpath and the green, it's OK. he takes the driver and once again miming impact, miming impact now waggle hitch and he creams it, he creams it, just creams it he does and it rolls, he rolls it up onto the apron, up onto the apron, rolls it onto the apron of the damn green, twenty feet from the pin, he almost reaches, almost reached the green, he'd had every right to wait, every right to be waiting, dawdling, I'm dizzy bit but now, he introduced himself as Bobby, and he could certainly have driven, easily driven the green, how could I have? I had no idea, no clue really, how could

I have? later on, he's not a particularly big kid, later on I end up, it's true, I end up, it's OK, and only now, only now can I see and hear it.

now I realize that it is my turn, my turn to finally hit, and I hear, well wait, not yet almost, I haven't hit yet now dizzy bit but it's almost my turn to hit, and I watch bobby's shot and I'm all "good shot" and he offers up an "I'll say!" and as if from afar, it's my turn now, I can, I can hear them. it's now my turn, my turn to hit and I can hear, I can hear them. I can hear them from far off and away. I hear a dinga dinga ding ding. I hear a dinga dinga ding ding. I hear them closing in closer now and I hear the bell dinga dinga ding ding, it's banging, baka daka dak dak dak. banging baka daka dak dak dak, dinga dinga ding ding ding ding ding, they're coming they are coming! they're back. baka daka ding ding dak dak dak my bell, my friends, my goodness me oh my so swift they do they do seem to be running, look at that, running for me from over the hill from over the hill from over the hill binga dinga ding dong, banging baka daka dak dak dak, dinga dinga ding ding ding ding ding. they feel me, they feel me, they feel the need, see and hear the need to intervene. they recognize that things are not proper, not going, not going well where we are, we're inside the head, inside my head stalled, I pause just stalled out ahead and dizzy bit but now my turn, my turn to hit, they're coming, I hear them ahead, I hurry, I need, I need to set up. I set up, I'm setting up. I'm starting now to set up.

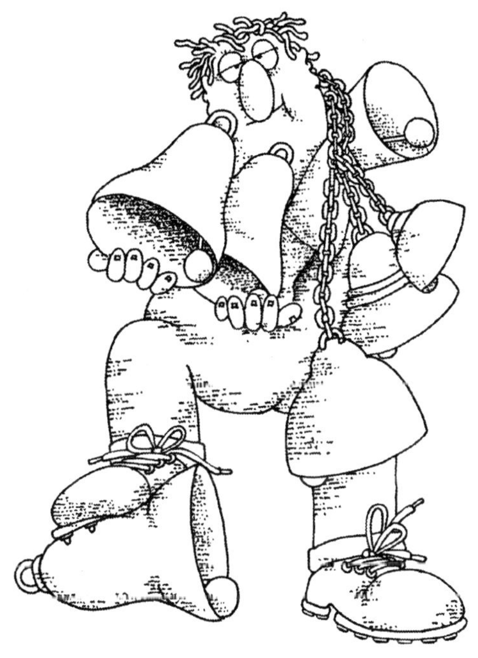

7.

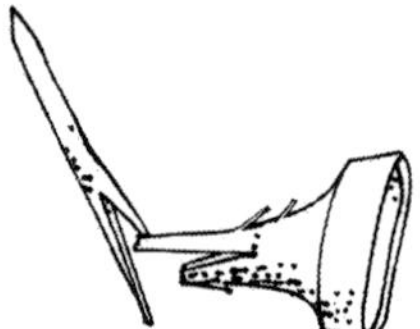

now I'm distraction, picturing the shape of the shot, I do picture the shape of the shot, but they see me distracted they know I'm distracted, I'm unfolding, have been for many minutes now and might not find focus, there's a target might not even, I need to set up, reset, start again, I'm distraught I thought, thinking I hear them with me, ponypuppykitty incoming, they're coming, running, descending strong and fast, descending quickly coming down upon to help us focus help me find a refined focus, help me concentrate on some such something, loud and proud, there's a target might not even, might be thinking on what is most, and we might ask what is most, most important, what is most important in movements of this nature, natural movements of this nature, this singular natural moment, this way, this kind of way they listen, can they listen to me? are they? are they hearing me thinking? they can, can they hear me thinking? are they listening to how I am thinking about my thinking? am I ready? there it is, ready? is the wind blowing or being blown? is the wind blown? does the wind blow? where is it?

now there's the target, big and bold, there's the target, a target I chose, I have chosen, I am starting to choose again, but you know they chose me. I hear banging gone baka daka dak dak dak, dinga dinga ding ding ding go go go, there it is and there it is, the target, and I waggle and I hear and I waggle and I am here.

now I waggle loose to hitch, too loose to hitch, there's a hitch and I begin, I begin to consider it, I'm beginning to consider to consider how quickly I am unfolding like this, like what's happening now. this connection, this sounding out sounds like sounds like a worry, I love a game, just love a game, oh how I love a game of hip action foot action knee action hip turn shoulder turn and pivot, I pivot. I love a game of total motion, I love a game of hip action foot action knee action hip turn shoulder turn and pivot, I pivot. I think over what I've begun. I love a game of total motion.

now I'm ready ready, but I pull away, I'm ready ready and I pull away, I do approach pre-routine, prepping, pre-waggle ready, I'm ready, I'm athletic ready, and I approach but I pull away, wait, hesitate, not ready. I pause not ready, now waggle waggle. I begin, I'm beginning to consider it's my turn to hit, I'm to hit, up to hit, it's my turn now, I move to take my turn. I should be considering position one, my wrist, my wrist and fingers considering a game of flyfishing, wristcock, I love a game of flyfishing, I love thinking about flyfishing, thinking about throwout action like, I'm like leaning, I'm leaning through a turn, there're three basic planes: there's floors, there's doors, and there's an inclined roof. there's a sweet spot sweet, there's a sweet spot, there's plumbobbing plum bobbing, you hold a club like that like this but do you really know what you're doing? bob it, you do, you know, there's steering like you're playing, like you're loving steering, I'm loving steering, I love a game of rolling the hoop, you roll a hoop? you're steering stationary, so very stationary, with a stationary head like a stationary head on a spinning skater, you feel it when you skate, you spin, you're skating, your right forearm draws a line between two points here and there, here and there.

now you spin, here and there, there's rhythm, here and there, there's a shaft and a crankshaft, there's connection, there's a crankshaft connection, shoulder turn and pivot, I pivot. there's resultant forces snipping much like a skip, like skipping rocks skip skip over water it does, they do, they skip over skip skip skip over the water. much like a skip, like skipping rocks.

now there's power, there's accumulation, they are quite powerful these accumulators, there's a stretching a stretching of a sling like a slingshot you know I consider it, consider stretching thinking of potential and kinetic energy like you might drop a hammer. I'm dropping a hammer, I drop a hammer right now, thinking I'm thinking of a plane line, my pivot center like a ball tethered to a pole, there's tetherball, a tetherball pole, I love a game of tetherball, I play a game, I'll play you, I would like to play you in a game of tetherball around a pole I would, there's a swift revolving door like a pivot like a pivot, there's walking, there's running and there's pacing.

now you're pacing you're pacing you've been pacing and running and walking yourself now we slow down quickly as we know we know all about momentum transfer like a

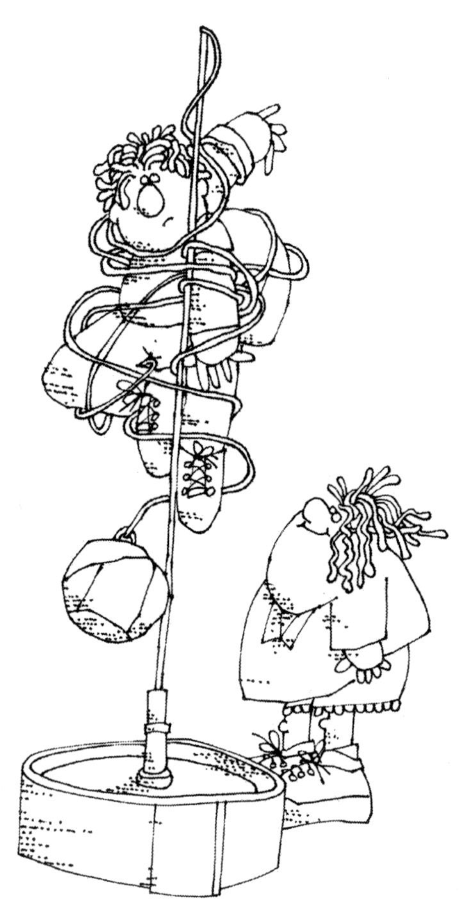

hammer thrower, I'm a hammer thrower, I love to throw hammers like a bullet hole, like a bullet hole through a baseball, you know all about momentum transfer, it does, like there's lines of compression and lever assemblies, or a nutcracker, you might you might find use for a cracker, you might have a nutcracker at home. there's laws, there's the burning, the burning of fuel, there's inclined planes and impact points, there's impact points like darts, like a cue ball is there, see it? maybe picking spots on a dart board, there's one, there's two and another. I'm thinking of impact intervals, and another, I'm thinking of impact always and I'm thinking of impact some more.

now I am bowling, I am thinking, thinking tenpins, oh how much I do love a game of tenpins, but where is impact as it relates to your body? your body is it. is the impact. it is the moment of you actually actually releasing the ball, right there there's release, there's thinking, there's asking, is it hitting or swinging? there's a catapult, and I pivot, you know you might have a, might have a catapult at home, there's the tension, a tension in the line, the pulling, the pulling or you're cutting, you're cutting it tense, the tense line, there's swinging there's swinging you're swinging the sling, the shot, slinging shots, the slingshot, I'm thinking of hinge action, I'm thinking of gyroscopic action, thinking of whirling a weight on a string, I'm thinking of whirling a weight on a string, I am thinking of what it is like to be whirling a weight on a string. I'm thinking of flying wedges, I'm thinking of the flat and the vertical, on the zont zont, multiple sailboats, multiple sails on multiple boats floating, they float, I'm thinking of floating horizontal with my left hand, I'm thinking of flat vertical wrist, I'm thinking of left left left, I left it, chop chop chop, you know it's endless, this endless belt, this endless belt effect, the endless belt effect like a like a like a duck ducks on a belt at a shooting gallery, you know like multiple sails on a sailboat, like ducks in a row, endless ducks in a row at a shooting gallery, I love a game of duck shooting endless belt effect.

now there's concentration, there's concentration, there's coefficient of restitution much like I'm thinking about how it's much like splashing water, I'm splashing water, I splash water. there it is, this concentration, there's club head throwaway, throwing the head, there's a club, there's throwaway. there's using a sickle, I love a game of using the sickle or scythe, I love a scythe, you know you go scythe a field, go swing a sickle, I love a game of harvesting the crop, you harvest the crop? using the sickle to harvest, that's the old game, that's the difference, difference between club head lag between club head lag and the throwaway, there's throwing rocks, there's rocks, there's throwing feathers, there's feathers. there's check rein action, you might have a dog, you might have a leash, you might check rein, you need to check rein, check rein, you need check rein action. there's check rein action.

now there's a center, there's a centrifugal force, I'm thinking of whirling of whirling a weight on a string, again I'm thinking of basic motions, I'm thinking of driving tacks, driving tacks like pins like brads like tapping tacks in place, I'm thinking of balance, I'm thinking of balance, I'm thinking of the dance, I'm thinking of being a hula dancer! I'm thinking of backspin, of backspin, I'm thinking of throwing a frisbee, I'm thinking of axis tilt, I'm thinking of tilting my axis as I lean and tilt, I'm thinking pointy, I'm thinking pointy, I'm pointy like an axe is sharp, so I'm holding an axe handle like a rope handle, I'm thinking of oh, there it is. you can ask yourself whether you're going dragging, I'm dragging, whether I'm gonna drag something or chop something? I want to chop on something, but I'm thinking of these associated planes.

now I'm open to thinking, thinking of a floor, I'm thinking of a door, I'm thinking of the floor and I'm thinking of the door. I'm open. I'm thinking of an arc, an arc of attack, I'm open to thinking of impact. always, thinking of impact as an arc, as movement, as an arc of attack, the arc of attack toward impact, the angle of approach, my thinking of impact can be low impact, low and slow, but could should be slow back fast through, slow back fast through, I thought. I'm thinking of angular motion, I'm thinking of going round, thinking of going round, I'm thinking of a merry-go-round, I'm thinking of going on a merry-go-round. now there's angular forces, I'm thinking of wrecking, I'm thinking of a wrecking ball, aiming, I'm aiming, there's a target far, there's a target near, there's targets plural, hear them? there's points, a wrecking ball, there's a bullseye, there it is. the address routine, pre-waggle, there it is. like you know I have an address routine, a preliminary address, preliminary routine I have, I do have, I have knee action, I have foot action, I've knee action, and I have foot action, I have really good foot action, I'm told, and there's balance. I'm told, I think. I punch it, my concentration, my concentration is on acceleration, and the question is good, the question is grand: can you, can you really punch harder, or can you, can you only punch faster? it is my turn to play these are the, slow back fast through, these are the, these are the, Shanking itself, to the top, Shanking itself is when, is when these, these are the things, these are the things thunk these are the the

now it is my turn, my turn, and now it is my turn, slow back… thwack!

oh no, oh it's it's supposed to go black, it's supposed to go black. no wait, it's ok, leave them up.

OK, I met, I met a pirate.

I met a pirate and she she told me, she told me about this new movie, new pirate movie, did you hear? have you heard about the new pirate movie?

it's rated PG-13.

or

OK, I met. I met another pirate.

I met a pirate, and she, I noticed, she had her ears pierced, I could see she had pierced ears, and I asked her, I asked her, "mam, how much did that cost? how much did it cost for you to get your ears pierced?"

she said she said, "a dollar an ear."

end of play

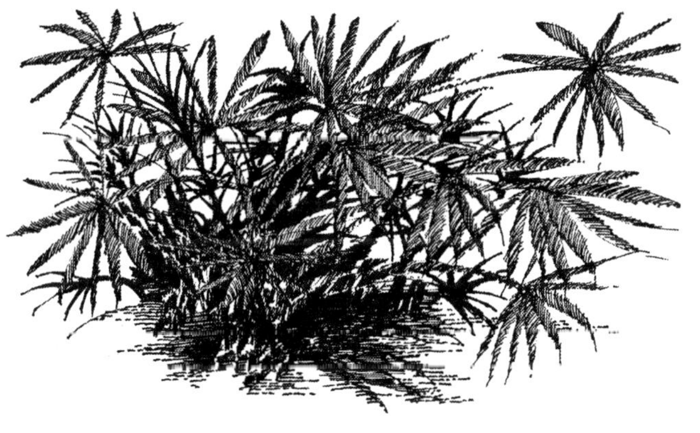

APPENDIX (Thanks Talullah)

position one

position two

position three (at the top)

position four

position four and a half

position four and a half (2)

position five (at impact)

Rob Erickson performs as lumberob. Rob is a writer and a performer and a musician and a student and a teacher and a father. His plays include *Bam Tourine*, *Vice-President Glambeaux*, *Lynchplay: Jimmer has a Jaw in a Jar*, *Gank Thod*, *Off the Hozzle*, *Hibiscus, Grapefruit, waternowater* (with Peter Glantz), *Always Talk to your Healthcare Provider*, *Stalled on the Kiddy Speed Display*, *Agro Expo 27* (with Stephanie Mankins), *The Sea Grass Analogy* (with Leslie Strongwater), *Jon Jon the Jon Cleaner* (with Kristin Erickson), *Scope and Sequence*, *Now My Know My, Yes My Do*, and *For We Trust We Have A Good Conscience*, among others on-going and not-going. In the past/present/future he has collaborated and performed with Nature Theater of Oklahoma, Jad Fair, Kevin Blechdom, Martha Colburn, Blectum from Blechdom, Peter Glantz, Laura Peterson, Kramer, Half Japanese, and ToonBox Entertainment. His ol' psych/punky/twangy band was called Adult Rodeo, which he founded with his wife in 1998. They made four full-length albums: *the kissyface*, *TEXXXAS*, *long-range rapid-fire*, and *Tough Titty*. Rob has a BA from Brown University in semiotics and performance theory, an MFA from Brooklyn College in playwriting, and a Masters of Science in Education from Metropolitan College. Currently, he teaches 8th grade honors humanities at Booker T. Washington Middle School in Manhattan. He lives in Brooklyn with his wife, Stephanie Mankins, and their absurdly superduper children, Tallulah and Finnegan. His is broken, lurching, shaky aesthetic – doing undoing.

Bob Erickson is a teacher and an artist. He's also Rob's dad. Bob has been a golf professional in South Florida for almost 40 years, and has been a professional illustrator for longer than that. A Carnegie-Mellon refugee, his editorial and comic work has appeared in numerous newspapers and magazines and on greeting card racks in both the United States and Europe. His canvases include the Palm Beach Post, Miami Herald, Golf Digest, Golf Magazine, and Roger Alan Studio Cards. He is renowned as an extraordinarily creative teacher of the game of golf, and he is sought after as a gifted tournament director. This is his first formal collaboration with Rob, and he takes no responsibility for his son's disturbed misunderstanding of basic swing theory. Bob lives in Port St. Lucie, FL with his wife, Rhea.

Illustrations by Bob Erickson
Back cover photograph © 2011 Jim Moore
Book design: Karinne Syers and Rob Erickson

53rd State Press publishes new plays, performance texts, and translations. Founded in 2007 by Karinne Keithley, it is now incorporated in the state of Illinois, and awaiting formal non-profit status. 53rd State Press is co-edited by Antje Oegel and Karinne (Keithley) Syers.

For more information, to order books, or to subscribe to the season catalog, please visit www.53rdstatepress.org

53rd State books are available to the trade through Small Press Distribution: www.spdbooks.org.

53SP 01 The Book of the Dog
53SP 02 Joyce Cho Plays
53SP 03 Nature Theater of Oklahoma's No Dice
53SP 04 Nature Theater of Oklahoma's Rambo Solo
53SP 05 When You Rise Up
53SP 06 Montgomery Park, or Opulence
53SP 07 Crime or Emergency
53SP 08 Off the Hozzle

Forthcoming from 53rd State in 2011-12: New writing by Erin Courtney, Kristen Kosmas, and Pig Iron Theatre Company.